Foreword

German Grammar for All derives from the "Grammar and Syntax" section of the **Advanced German Grammar Course**. This new volume now provides a small, easy to use and very practical reference to all students interested in finding out about German grammar.

German Grammar for All gives help with the syntactical, semantic and stylistic problems that arise in translating from English into German. It also includes, however, a good deal of idiomatic material, as well as the sort of information that will help students to grasp the meaning and function of prefixes and suffixes and thus enable them to enlarge considerably their vocabulary.

The idea for this book came from a chance remark from a teacher who asked that the very practical reference part of the **Advanced German Course** should be available in this new form.

I am grateful to that teacher for the suggestion.

L.J. Russon

Chandlers Ford 1988

German Grammar for All

A. RUSSON and L.J. RUSSON M.A.

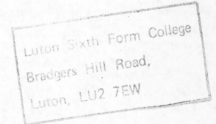

LONGMAN

Longman Group UK Limited
Longman House, Burnt Mill, Harlow, Essex CM20 2JE, England
and Associated Companies throughout the World.

First published 1989
Second impression 1992
ISBN 0 582 04006 X

Set in Ehrhardt 9/11pt

Produced by Longman Group (FE) Ltd
Printed in Hong Kong

Abbreviations and Signs Used

A	accusative; governs accusative
AD	governs accusative and dative
adj.	adjective
adv.	adverb
AG	governs accusative and genitive
cf.	compare
D	dative; governs dative
e.g.	for example
etc.	etcetera
F.	familiar
f.	feminine
fig.	figurative meaning
G	genitive; governs genitive
i.e.	that is
imp.	impersonal
intr.	intransitive
irr.	irregular verb
Lit.	literary
m.	masculine
N	nominative
n.	neuter
o.s.	oneself
pl.	plural
s.	strong verb
s.b.	somebody
sing.	singular
s.th.	something
tr.	transitive
*	conjugated with *sein*
(*)	conjugated with *sein* or *haben* according to the meaning
⁄	indicates that the syllable so marked is stressed
×	indicates that the syllable so marked is unstressed
-	inserted between the prefix and verb indicates that the verb is separable

1 Word Order in Main Clauses

(a) In the **main clause** (statements) the finite verb is, with very few exceptions (see (*d*), (*e*) and (*f*) below), always the **second** idea. Unless there are other considerations such as special emphasis, emotional intensity, etc., the past participle, the infinitive(s), the separable verbal prefix (but see 6(*g*)*ii*) and the verbal complement will come last.

1	2			
Er	hat	ihr	einige Zeit zum Besinnen	gelassen.
Wir	werden	also	zusammen	arbeiten.
Du	kannst	sie	eine halbe Stunde draußen	spazierenfahren.
Ich	will	sie	alle um mich	haben.
Sie	marschieren	oft	an meinem Fenster	vorbei.
Sie	hatten	ihn	eine Woche lang	zu Besuch.

(b) The finite verb may be preceded by any **one** of the following: the subject (noun, pronoun or noun clause or phrase), the introductory *es*, the object (noun, pronoun (except *es*) or noun clause or phrase), an adverb or adverbial phrase or adverbial clause, a present or past participle or participial phrase, an infinitive, a predicative adjective or a separable verbal prefix.

It does not, however, follow that any word order will do, provided the finite verb is the second idea. The placing of any word(s) except the noun or pronoun subject before the verb tends to give it (or them) special emphasis or sometimes emotional intensity, which in every case must be justified by the context.

The noun or pronoun subject preceding the verb normally carries no particular stress. If it is desired to give the noun subject more weight a position last in the clause is sometimes a very effective way of doing this.

1	2			
Der Zug	kam	pünktlich	in Hannover	an.
Daß er da ist,	muß	ein Geheimnis		bleiben.
So etwas zu behaupten	ist			unerhört.
Es	ist	niemand		da.

1	2		
Meinen Bruder	habe ich	dort	getroffen.
Den	kenne ich		nicht.
Daß er krank war,	wußte ich		schon.
„Ja",	sagte er		zu ihm.
„Ich kann nicht kommen",	sagte sie		traurig.
Gern	hätte ich	ihm	geholfen.
Am nächsten Morgen	fühlte er	sich	krank.
Als er zurückkam,	fand er	niemand	zu Hause.
Suchend	blickte er	sich	um.
Bestraft	muß er		werden!
Auf die Folter gespannt,	gestand er		alles.
Gewinnen	müssen wir		unbedingt.
Arbeiten	tut er		nie.
Still	war es		ringsum.
Fort	ging er!		
Außerordentlich förderlich für das Aussagevermögen einer Sprache	ist	neben dem Wortvorrat die freie Wortstellung (W. SCHNEIDER).	

(c) The first element of the main clause, provided it remains a single entity, can be amplified at will. This can be done, if the clause begins with a noun or pronoun, by means of appositional or attributive phrases or clauses, or by relative clauses; and also by adverbs, adverbial phrases or adverbial clauses or relative clauses if the clause begins with an adverbial expression

1	2	
Das anhaltend gellende Klingeln, das Zeichen zum Beginn der Montagsandacht,	schlug	an sein Ohr (T. MANN).
Ich als ältester Sohn	habe	allein das Recht darauf.
Der Mann, seines Lebens nicht sicher,	suchte	bei Freunden seine Zuflucht.
Onkel Justus, galant wie er war,	schritt	ihr entgegen (T. MANN).
Kinder, solange sie schweigen,	mag	ich gern leiden.
Der Zug, den ich nehmen wollte,	kam	pünktlich an.
Der Koffer da	gehört	mir.
Am nächsten Morgen, als er aufwachte,	fühlte	er sich schon besser.
Durch den Anblick des lieben Gottes, der doch eine Weile alles in bleichen Schrecken versetzte,		

1	2
indem er mit fürchterlichem Brummen nach verschiedenen Richtungen auf das Butterbrot-papier zeigte, das hie und da auf den Fliesen lag,	war Kai in vorzügliche Laune geraten (T. MANN).

(d) In questions introduced by an interrogative (*wo? wer?* etc.) and in the 3rd person imperative the finite verb is the second idea; in questions not introduced by an interrogative and in first and second person imperative forms the finite verb comes **first**.

Was **hat** er gesagt?   Man **nehme** sechs Eier!
But **Hat** er schon geantwortet?   **Gehen** wir! **Gehen** Sie nach Hause!

(e) In main clauses expressing a wish the finite verb comes **first**.

Wären wir doch zu Hause!

(f) In exclamations introduced by *wie, was für, welcher*, etc., the verb most commonly comes **last** (see *82*).

Wie blaß du **aussiehst**!   Was für ein Mann das **war**!

(g) Interjections, *ja* and *nein*, and words and phrases that are separated by a comma from the beginning of the German sentence like *nun, im Gegenteil, kurz, kurzum, mit einem Wort* and, occasionally also, *gewiß, freilich, allerdings* and *immerhin* are treated as being outside the main clause and as therefore not affecting the word order.

Ach! das **ist** wahr. Nein, das **glaube** ich nicht.
Im Gegenteil, ich **bin** gefahren. Mit einem Wort, du **bist** verrückt.
Freilich, da **kann** man nichts sagen.

(h) In the Volkslied and in poetry akin to it in spirit the finite verb often comes first. The finite verb is also to be found in poetry coming at the end of the main clause.

Liegt eine Stadt im Tale (DEHMEL).
Am Fenster ich einsam stand (EICHENDORFF).
Ein Schweigen in schwarzen Wipfeln wohnt (TRAKL).

2 Word Order in Compound Sentences

In a compound sentence, i.e. a sentence consisting of two or more main clauses, the finite verb is the **second** idea in each of the clauses. The main clauses may be (and usually are, if there are only two) linked by co-ordinating conjunctions (7).

	1	2		1	2		
	Er	legte sich hin	und	(er)	schlief	bald	ein.
	Er	legte sich hin,	und	bald	schlief	er	ein.
	Er	legte sich hin,	denn	er	war	müde.	

	1	2		1	2		1	2
Er	zog sich aus,	(er)	legte sich hin	und	(er)	schlief ein.

NOTE: The subject, if it is the same as in the first clause, may be omitted after *und, aber* and *sondern* in the subsequent clause(s), provided no other word precedes the verb.

3 Word Order in Subordinate Clauses

(a) In subordinate clauses which begin either with a subordinating conjunction (*8 (a)*), an interrogative (*8 (b)*) or a relative pronoun (*46*) the finite verb normally comes **last** in the subordinate clause (i). If the verb is a separable verb its prefix immediately precedes it and is attached to it (ii). The past participle or infinitive immediately precedes the finite verb (iii).

i Während er so in seinem Buch **las**, ...
ii Obgleich sie gar nicht so häßlich **aus**sah, ...
iii Der Mann, der zuerst ins Zimmer **getreten** war, ...
Sie fragte, wie er **geschlafen** habe.
Da er endlich ins Zimmer **kommen** mußte, ...

(b) *Exceptions:*

i When there are two or more infinitives in the clause the finite auxiliary verb (*haben* or *werden*) normally immediately precedes them.

Der Tag wird kommen, an dem sie das **werden** tun müssen.
Das Buch, das er **hatte** drucken lassen, ...
Wenn er das **hätte** wissen können, ...

ii When a verb in the main clause introduces direct speech the finite verb comes second in the subordinate clause.

Er sagte: ,,Ich **gehe** jetzt nach Hause."

iii When a verb in the main clause introduces indirect speech without *daß* the finite verb comes second in the subordinate clause.

Er sagte, er **sei** sehr müde.
Er sagte, sie **solle** sofort zu Bett gehen.
But Er sagte, daß er sehr müde sei.

iv When *wenn* is omitted in conditional clauses the finite verb comes first.

Hätte er den Brief gelesen, so... (*if he had read*).

4

v When *ob* or *wenn* are omitted in *als ob* or *als wenn* clauses the finite verb immediately follows *als*.

Er tat, als **wüßte** er nichts davon.

But Er tat, als ob er nichts davon wüßte.

4 Word Order in Complex Sentences

(a) In complex sentences (i.e. in sentences consisting of one or more main clauses and one or more subordinate clauses) the main clause may (i) precede the subordinate clause(s); (ii) follow the subordinate clause(s); (iii) enclose the subordinate clause(s). The subordinate clause may itself (iv) enclose one or more subordinate clauses.

i   Er sagte sofort, daß er es tun würde, wenn er Zeit hätte.
ii Nachdem er sich hingelegt hatte und eingeschlafen war, klopfte es.
iii Er wollte den Brief, der eben gekommen war und den er schnell gelesen hatte, sofort beantworten.
iv Er sagte sofort, daß, wenn er Zeit hätte, er es tun würde.

(b) It is often stylistically preferable to complete one clause before starting the next, especially when the sentence would otherwise end haltingly or become too involved.

Er las den Brief **durch**, der eben gekommen war und auf den er so lange und sehnsüchtig gewartet hatte.

Ich werde ihm das Buch **geben**, das ich ihm versprochen habe.

Er sagte, daß er ein Haus **gekauft habe**, das mitten in einem Wald stehe.

5 Word Order in Concessive Clauses

After a concessive clause introduced by conjunctions such as *was ... auch*, *welcher ... auch, wie/so ... auch* and also by *ob ... ob/oder, sei es (daß) ... sei es (daß)* there is usually no inversion of the subject and verb in the main clause.

Welche Talente er auch besitzen mochte, er konnte ... (*whatever talents*). In welcher Richtung man auch reisen mag, man ... (*in whichever direction*).

Wie/so schön sie auch sein mag, sie ist ... (*beautiful though she is*).

Ob es regnet oder nicht, ich gehe jeden Tag spazieren.

NOTE: One occasionally meets the same construction after a *wenn*-clause Students are, however, not advised to adopt this practice.   ·

Wenn mich die Welt so fragen wird, es wird schwer sein ... (KAFKA).

6 Word Order within the Clause

(a) In a main clause the weakest element tends to come immediately after the finite verb, in a subordinate clause immediately after the introductory word. The stronger the element, the closer it will tend to come to the end of both main and subordinate clause.

In the following sections dealing with word order within the clause this principle should always be borne in mind; for if a word or phrase normally spoken without stress is given particular significance it will then tend to come later in the clause than it would otherwise have done.

(b) **Direct and Indirect Objects**

If there are two noun objects in a clause the indirect (dative) normally precedes the direct (accusative). If there are two personal pronoun objects, the direct normally precedes the indirect. But any pronoun object will normally precede a noun object. (Note that the second of the two objects has the greater stress.)

Er gab dem Mann das **Buch.**
Er gab es **ihm.** Geben Sie es **mir!**
Er gab ihm das **Buch.** Er gab es dem **Mann.** Er hat das meinem **Freund** gesagt.

However, emphasis would require one to say:

Er hat mir **das** gesagt. Ich bringe dir **ihn** (= den Koffer).
Er gab den Apfel seiner **Schwester** (und nicht seinem Bruder).
Er zieht das Land der **Stadt** vor.

(c) **The Prepositional Object**

The prepositional object normally follows other objects.

Er schrieb den Brief an meinen Bruder.

(d) **The Reflexive Pronoun and the Personal Pronoun Object**

i In the main clause the reflexive pronoun or the personal pronoun object immediately follows the finite verb except when there is inversion of verb and pronoun subject.

Er setzte sich/ihn auf den Stuhl.
Er hat sich/ihn auf den Stuhl gesetzt.
Dann setzte sich mein Vater. Dann setzte sie mein Vater auf einen Stuhl. Dann gab ihr mein Vater einen Trunk Wasser.
But Dann setzte er sich. Dann setzte er sie auf einen Stuhl.

ii In a subordinate clause it is considered more correct for the reflexive pronoun or personal pronoun object to come immediately before the noun subject of the clause, though many modern writers place it after the noun subject. If the subject of the clause is a pronoun the pronoun object or reflexive pronoun comes immediately after it.

Da sich mein Bruder jetzt erholt hat, ...
Wenn mich die Welt so fragen wird, ...
But Da er sich jetzt erholt hat, ... Wenn er mir so antwortet, ...

iii *Es* (accusative) precedes the dative reflexive pronoun, unless it is contracted to *'s*, when it is attached to it.

Stell es dir vor! Stellen Sie es sich vor!
But Stell dir's vor! Stellen Sie sich's vor!

(e) **Nicht**

i In a negative main clause *nicht* immediately precedes the past participle, infinitive(s), separable prefix, predicative adjective or noun, or adverb or adverbial phrase of place, manner or degree. If none of these is present *nicht* is the last word.

Ich habe ihn nicht gesehen.
Du kannst ihn heute nicht sehen.
Du brauchst nicht zu kommen.
Du hättest es nicht sagen sollen.
Sehen Sie sich jetzt nicht um!
Es ist heute nicht kalt.
Das ist nicht mein Mann.
Er ist heute nicht in der Schule.
Ich bin nicht zu Fuß gekommen.
Ich mag ihn nicht sehr.
Ich sehe ihn nicht. Vergessen Sie mich nicht!
Ohne diese Erkenntnis hilft aller gute Wille nicht.

ii In a negative subordinate clause *nicht* precedes the finite verb. If there is a past participle, one or more infinitives, a predicative adjective or noun, or an adverb or adverbial phrase of place, manner or degree in the clause *nicht* precedes these.

Wenn ich es nicht tue, ...
Wenn ich es nicht getan hätte, ...
Wenn Sie nicht kommen können, ...
Wenn Sie nicht hätten kommen können, ...
Wenn es heute nicht kalt wäre, ...
Da er nicht mein Sohn ist, ...
Obgleich er noch nicht da ist, ...
Da ich nicht zu Fuß gekommen bin, ...
Da er heute nicht genug gearbeitet hat, ...

iii If a particular word in the clause is to be negatived *nicht* immediately precedes that word.

Ich mag sie sehen, aber nicht **ihn**.
Ich habe nicht **ihn** gesehen, sondern seinen Bruder.
Komm nicht **heute**, komm lieber morgen!

7

(f) Adverbs and Adverbial Phrases

i   The order of adverbs or adverbial phrases within the clause tends to be as follows: (1) cause, (2) time, (3) manner, (4) place, (5) purpose or result, (6) degree. The underlying principle, which generally accounts for this order, as well as for deviations from it, is that the more intimately an adverbial expression is linked with the finite verb, the further away it stands from it in the main clause (and the closer to it in the subordinate clause).

Er trat|heute morgen|ganz unerwartet|ins Zimmer.
Als er|heute morgen|ganz unerwartet|ins Zimmer|trat, ...
Sie marschierten|oft|mit Fahnen und Musik und Gesang|an meinem Fenster|vorbei (DÖBLIN).
Wir mußten|wegen des weiten Weges|sofort|nach Hause|zur Klavierstunde|gehen.
Ich habe|heute nachmittag|im Garten|nur wenig|geschafft.

ii It is often possible to avoid too many adverbial expressions coming together by beginning the sentence with the one or other of them that is not intimately linked with the verb.

Heute morgen trat er ganz unerwartet ins Zimmer.
Ganz unerwartet trat er heute morgen ins Zimmer.

iii If there are several adverbial expressions of time or of place the more general tends to come first.

Er kommt jeden Morgen um 9 Uhr.
Der Hund liegt draußen im Garten vor der Tür.

iv Two or more place adverbs or two or more time adverbs coming at the beginning of the sentence may be looked upon as constituting one idea only (cf. 1(c)).

Eines Abends, Ende Mai, klopfte es wieder an ihrer Tür (RINSER).
Draußen im Garten vor dem Haus liegt der Hund.

v   The adverb(ial expression), unless it comes first in the sentence, is preceded by all direct and indirect pronoun objects (cf. 6(a)), but usually stands between two noun objects, and comes before a prepositional object, a single noun object and a predicative adjective.

Gestern hat er sich sehr amüsiert.
Er hat sich gestern sehr amüsiert.
Ich habe es ihm gestern gegeben.
But Ich habe meiner Schwester gestern das Buch gegeben.
Ich habe gestern mit ihr gesprochen.
Ich habe gestern meinen Freund getroffen.
Ich habe es gestern meinem Freund gesagt.
Sie sah gestern sehr blaß aus.

(g) **The Prefix of Separable Verbs** (cf. 60 (*f-k*))

i In the present and imperfect tenses of main clauses and in the imperative the prefix of separable verbs comes last.

Er geht um 8 Uhr **aus**. Er ging um 8 Uhr **aus**.
Geh doch **aus**!

NOTE: Occasionally, and then usually in poetry (but see *1(b)*), the separable prefix precedes the verb (and is sometimes attached to it) in the simple tenses of main clauses.

Auf tat sich das Licht (GOETHE).
Aufflattern weiße Vögel (TRAKL).

ii Separable verbs are in all other cases written as one word, the prefix coming first.

Als er gestern **ausging**, ... Er ist schon **ausgegangen**.
Er wollte **ausgehen**. Er wagte nicht **auszugehen**.

(h) **Deviations from Normal Word Order**

i In comparisons the incomplete clause dependent on *als* or *wie* usually follows the clause with which it is compared.

Gestern hat es weniger geregnet als heute.
Gestern hat es nicht so viel geschneit wie heute.
Da er viel älter ist als ich, ... Da er ebenso alt ist wie ich, ...

ii Both in main clauses and in subordinate clauses a phrase that would normally precede the verb will sometimes be found to follow it. This occurs quite often in conversation; but it is also met with in careful writing when the sentence is deliberately dislocated in order to point a meaning more clearly, or sometimes to avoid too remote an antecedent of a relative clause.

Es kann **bedeuten** Begriff oder Vorstellung oder Gedanke oder Einfall (W. SCHNEIDER).
Dichtung hat nur dem etwas zu schenken, der empfangbereit **ist** für ihre Gaben (W. SCHNEIDER).
Er tat es nicht, weil er einen Brief bekommen **hatte** von seiner Mutter, die ihm davon abriet (DRACH).

(i) **Parenthetical Clauses**

There is inversion of verb and subject only in the short parenthetical clause.

Er ist, glaube ich, höchst intelligent.
Eine Dame, heißt es, könne ...
But Er ist – ich habe es mehr als einmal gesagt – höchst intelligent.

(j) For the position of the present and past participles in participial phrases, see 64(*b*).

7 Co-ordinating Conjunctions

(a) All six co-ordinating conjunctions – *und, oder, sondern, aber, denn, allein* (= *but*, in literary use only) – link clauses without affecting the word order.

Er kann heute nicht kommen, denn er ist viel zu müde.
Als er ins Zimmer trat und mich sah, wurde er blaß.

(b) The first three – *und, oder* and *sondern* – also link nouns, pronouns, adjectives, etc., with one another; and *aber* can be used to link adjectives.

Du und ich; ihr Bruder oder ihre Schwester; nicht schön, sondern häßlich; er ist klug, aber faul.

8 Subordinating Conjunctions and Interrogatives

Subordinating conjunctions and subordinating interrogatives send the finite verb to the end of the clause.

(a) Subordinating Conjunctions

als	*when, as, than*	falls	
als ob; als wenn	*as if, as though*	für den Fall	
angenommen, daß	*supposing that*	daß	*in case, if*
(an-)statt daß	*instead of*	im Falle, daß	
	(+ gerund)	indem	*while, as, by (+*
auch wenn	*even if*		*gerund)*
auf daß	*so that (purpose)*	indes(-sen)	*while, as*
ausgenommen, daß	*except that*	in dem Maße,	*(in proportion)*
außer daß		wie	*as*
ausgenommen, wenn	*unless, except when*	in gleichem Maße, wie	*to the same extent as*
außer wenn		insofern	*in so far as,*
		insoweit	*according as*
außer im Falle, daß	*except when, unless*	insofern ..., als	*in so far ... as*
bevor; ehe	*before*	je nachdem (wie)	*according as*
bis	*until, by the time that*	jedesmal, wenn	*whenever*
da	*as, since (causal)*	kaum daß	*(preceding main clause)*
dadurch, daß	*by (+ gerund)*		*no sooner ...*
damit	*so that (purpose)*		*than, hardly*
damit ... nicht	*unless, lest*		*... when*
daß	*that*		*(following main clause)*
es sei denn, daß	*unless*		*hardly (result)*
erst als	*not until, only when*		
erst wenn			

nachdem	after
nicht eher, (als) bis	not until
nun (,da)	now that
ob ..., ob/oder	whether ... or
obgleich	
obschon	
obwohl	*although*
obzwar	
ohne daß	without (+ gerund)
sei es, daß ...	whether ... or
sei es, daß ...	(whether)
seit(-dem)	since (temporal)
so ... auch (immer)	however (+ adjective or adverb)
sobald; sowie	as soon as
so daß	so that (result)
sofern; soweit	as/so far as
sofern nur	if only, as long as
solange	as long as
sooft	whenever
so sehr ... auch (immer)	however much (+ verb)
soviel	as far as
trotzdem	despite the fact that, although
um so (+ comparative) als	all the (+ comparative) because
ungeachtet (daß)	although
unter der Bedingung, daß	on condition that
vorausgesetzt, daß	provided that
während	while, whereas

wann ... (auch) immer	whenever
was ... auch (immer)	whatever (= pronoun)
was für ... auch	whatever (+ noun)
weil	because
welcher ... auch	whichever
wenn	if, when (-ever)
wenn ... auch	even if
wenn ... (erst) einmal	once
wenn ... nicht	unless
wenngleich	
wennschon	*although*
wer ... auch (immer)	whoever
wie	as (manner, time), how, when
wie ... auch (immer)	however (+ adj. or adv.)
wie sehr ... auch (immer)	however (+ verb)
wiewohl	although
wo ... auch (immer)	wherever
wohin ... auch (immer)	wherever, in whatever direction
wogegen	
wohingegen	*whereas*
zu ..., als daß	too (+ adjective or adverb) for (+ gerund)
zumal (,da)	especially as

NOTE 1: *Auf daß, indes(-sen), ungeachtet* are literary or archaic as conjunctions.

NOTE 2: In older German *obgleich, obschon, obwohl, obzwar, wenngleich* and *wennschon* were often separated by the subject.

Ob er gleich krank war, ...

NOTE 3: Only *obgleich, obschon,* etc., *wenn (auch), ob ... ob/oder* and *weil* can be used in phrases without a verb.

Obgleich arm, führt er ein volles Leben.

Ob jung oder alt, man gibt nie die Hoffnung auf.

Seine persönliche Gestalt ist, weil schwer faßbar ..., stark verschattet worden (S.ZWEIG).

(b) Interrogative Adverbs, Pronouns and Adjectives introducing Indirect Questions

ob	*whether, if*	welcher	*which*
wann	*when*	wer	*who*
warum, weshalb	*why*	wo	*where*
wie	*how, what ... like*	woher	*where from*
wieviel	*how much, how many*	wohin	*where to*
		womit	*with what*
wie viele	*how many*	worein	*into what*
wie lange	*how long*	worin	*in what*
was	*what*	wozu	*for what purpose*
was für	*what (sort of), which*	etc.	

9 Some difficult Conjunctions

(a) as:

Während (= *while*) er sich setzte, half ich ihm.
Da (= *since*) er krank ist, liegt er im Bett.
Als/wie (= *when*) er hereinkommt, stolpert er. (*Historic present*)
Als (= *when*) er hereinkam, stolperte er.
Wie (= *when*) er hereinkam, stolperte er. (*More colloquial*)
Wie (= *just as*) sie langsam auf mich zukam, ging ich ihr einen Schritt entgegen.
Er schreibt, wie (= *in the same way as*) er spricht.
Er zählte das Geld, wie (= *at the same time as*) er es aus den Taschen kramte.
In dem Maße wie (= *in proportion as*) das Hochwasser anwuchs, vergrößerte sich die allgemeine Unruhe.
Wie (= *in the way*) es manchmal geschieht, hörten wir die Vögel ganz deutlich.
Wie (= *as*, i.e. *which fact*) du weißt, bin ich jetzt allein.
Das Wetter verschlechterte sich, je weiter (= *the further*) sie nach Norden fuhren.
Genau so wie (= *just as*) der Fluß sich windet, genau so läuft der Weg daneben.
Indem er das sagte (= *saying that*), drehte er sich um.

(b) but:

Es ist nicht kalt, aber (= *however*) ich friere.
Sie ist nicht mehr jung, sondern (= *but on the contrary*) alt.
Er ist nicht nur reich, sondern steinreich.
Dort war nichts (weiter/anderes) als (= *except*) Unkraut.
Das ist alles andere als (= *anything but*) wahr.
Er ist nichts weniger als/alles andere als (= *anything but*) höflich.

(c) **since**:

Da (= *as*) er noch jung ist, benimmt er sich schlecht.
Seit(-dem) (= *now that he is*) er wieder gesund ist, geht er jeden Tag schwimmen.
Zwanzig Jahre war(en) es nun, daß (*or* seit) (=*since the time*) sie dort lebten.

(d) **so that**:

Wechsele deinen Platz, damit (= *in order that*) ich besser sehen kann.
Ich wechselte meinen Platz, so daß (= *with the result that*) ich ihn jetzt sehen konnte.
Er ist sehr beschäftigt, kaum daß man (= *so that one hardly*) ihn jetzt sieht.

(e) **when**:

Wenn er kommt, könnt ihr gehen. } *(Reference to future*
Wenn es geklingelt hat, könnt ihr gehen. } *event.)*
Wenn (= *whenever*) er vorbeigeht, grüßt er mich immer.
Als/wie (= *when, historic present*) er endlich vorbeigeht, grüßt er mich.
Wenn (= *whenever*) er vorbeiging, grüßte er mich immer.
Jedesmal wenn/sooft (= *whenever*) er daran dachte, lächelte er.
Als/wie (= *when, on one occasion*) er vorbeiging, grüßte er mich.
Als/nachdem/sobald (= *after, as soon as*) er seine Rede beendet hatte, setzte er sich.
Wann (= *when, direct question*) kommt er?
Wir wissen nicht, wann (= *when, indirect question*) er kommt.
Kaum war er aufgestanden, als man anfing, ihn auszupfeifen.
Kaum war er aufgestanden, so/da fing man an, ihn auszupfeifen.
Kaum daß er aufgestanden war, so/da fing man an, ihn auszupfeifen.
Der Tag kam, an dem (*or* wo *or* da (= *literary style*)) sie das Haus verlassen mußten.
Der Augenblick kam, in dem (*or* wo *or* da (= *literary style*)) sie es ihm sagen mußte.

(f) **while**:

Während (= *all the time during which*) er in Berlin lebte, ging er oft ins Theater.
Während (= *at one moment while*) er mit mir sprach, kam seine Frau auf uns zu.
Er blieb stehen, während (= *whereas*) ich einen Schritt weiter ging.
Indem er sich leicht verbeugte (= *bowing*), küßte er ihr die Hand. (*Same subject in both clauses.*)

10 Adverbial Conjunctions

also; so; daher; darum	} *therefore, and so*	deswegen deshalb	} *that is (the reason) why*

auch	*also, too, and*	folglich	
auch ... nicht	*nor, neither, not either*	infolgedessen	*consequently*
außerdem		indes(-sen)	
ferner	*besides, moreover, in addition, further*	unterdessen	*meanwhile*
überdies		kaum	*hardly, scarcely*
übrigens		nichtsdesto- weniger	*nevertheless*
zudem		sonst	*otherwise, or else*
besonders	*especially, particularly*	(so-)wie auch	*as well as*
namentlich		sowieso	*anyhow, as it is*
da	*then, so*	trotzdem	*in spite of that, all the same*
dennoch			
(je-)doch	*yet, nevertheless*	und zwar	*in fact, to be precise*
gleichwohl			

Examples:

Auch wußte er nichts davon. Ich auch nicht (*nor did I*). Sie malt Bilder, und zwar Landschaftsbilder. Obgleich er jedoch nichts davon wußte, ... (*However, although ...*)

NOTE: When adverbial conjunctions begin a sentence, inversion of subject and verb is usual; after *doch* there is inversion normally only in literary style.
Außerdem bin ich zu müde. Deshalb haben wir nicht angerufen.
But Doch es geht mich nichts an (P. WEISS).

11 Correlative Conjunctions

etwas anderes ... etwas anderes ⎱	*one thing ... another thing*
ein anderes/eines ... ein anderes ⎰	
bald ... bald	*now ... now*
ebenso ... wie	*just as much ... as*
einerseits ... and(e)rerseits	*on the one hand ... on the other*
entweder ... oder	*either ... or*
(genau) wie ... (genau) so	*as ... so*
gerade so wie ... so	*as ... so*
in gleichem Maße wie ... so	*as ... so*
je (+ comparative) ... desto/um so	*the ... the*
nicht ... noch	*not ... nor*
nicht genug (*or* nur wenig *or* kaum) ... geschweige denn	*not enough* (or *few* or *hardly*) ... *let alone*
sei es ... sei es	*whether ... or*
sowohl ... als/wie auch	*both ... and*
teils ... teils	*partly ... partly*
weder ... noch	*neither ... nor*
zwar ... aber/(je-)doch	*it is true ... but/yet*

Examples:

Etwas anderes/ein anderes/eines ist es, in einem Land zu reisen, **etwas anderes/ein anderes** (ist es), Land und Leute wirklich kennenzulernen.
Er wird sich **ebenso** gelangweilt haben, **wie** ich mich gelangweilt habe.
Entweder du gehst (gehst du *is less emphatic*) zu ihm, **oder** er kommt zu dir. **Entweder** er wird **oder** ich werde ihn sehen. **Entweder** sein Vater **oder** seine Mutter **wird** kommen.
Er hat es **nicht** getan, **noch** weiß er, wer es getan hat.
Es gibt sehr **wenig** Lehrer, **geschweige denn** Mathematiklehrer.
Je weiter wir vorwärts kamen, **desto** öder wurde die Landschaft.
Weder er hat geschrieben, **noch** sie hat von sich hören lassen. (*Different subjects in the two clauses.*) **Weder** hat er geschrieben, **noch** ist er zu uns gekommen. (*Same subject in both clauses*) **Weder** er **noch** ich **haben** ihn gesehen. **Weder** von ihm **noch** von seiner Mutter habe ich etwas gehört.
Ich habe nichts gehört, **weder** von ihm **noch** von seiner Mutter (*either ...
or*).
Wie's kommt, **so** wird's gegessen.

12 The Definite and Indefinite Articles

(a) For declension, see *87, 88*.

(b) Examples of deviation from English usage:

i Where English omits the article:

Der Mensch ist sterblich; die Zeit vergeht schnell (i.e. *in generalising statements*).
Der junge Karl; das protestantische Deutschland.
Der Bodensee (*Lake Constance*); der Mont Blanc; in der Schillerstraße; auf dem Humboldtplatz.
Im Sommer, im Mai, am Mittwoch, nach dem Frühstück.
Die Schweiz, die Türkei, die Tschechoslowakei, die Bretagne (*i.e. with feminine names of countries and provinces*); *but also:* der Harz, der Breisgau, das Elsaß. (*But* Elsaß-Lothringen (*Alsace-Lorraine*).)
In der Schule, in der Stadt, im Bett, aus dem Bett; zur Schule, zur Kirche, zur Arbeit gehen; mit der Post/Bahn, mit dem Auto/Zug/Schiff/Flugzeug kommen (*by post, etc.*).
An den Masern (*measles*), Windpocken (*chicken-pox*), am Mumps erkranken; an der Schwindsucht (*consumption*), am Krebs (*cancer*), an den Pocken (*small-pox*) sterben.

ii Where German omits the definite article:

Nach Verlauf mehrerer Stunden; zu Anfang/Beginn des Jahres; gegen Ende des Monats; seit Beendigung des Kriegs; Anfang Juni (*at the beginning of June*); Mitte Juli; Ende August.

Nach Norden; gegen Süden.
Wir waren bei Beneckes (*at the Benecke's*).
Folgende Zitate; aus obigem Grunde.

iii   Where German omits the indefinite article:

Er ist Engländer, sie ist Ausländerin; er will Ingenieur werden; er war nie Minister gewesen. (*But:* Er ist ein reicher Engländer.)
Ich als alter Arzt; er diente als Lehrer; er war als Bauer verkleidet (*disguised as a*).
Er hat guten Appetit; er hat Fieber (*a temperature*); er hat Kopfschmerzen, Halsschmerzen; wir haben Besuch (*a visitor/visitors*); er hat große/keine Eile (*is in a great/in no hurry*).
Er spricht mit leiser, lauter Stimme; er ist (in) guter, schlechter Laune/Stimmung; er ist anderer Meinung/Ansicht; es kam zu Ende.

iv   Where German omits the partitive (*some, any*):

Hast du Butter? Ja, ich habe Butter. Ich esse nie Butter.
Er ißt vom (*some of the*) Brot, er trinkt vom Wein.

v   Where English uses the indefinite article, German the definite:

2 Mark das Kilo, 3 Schilling das Pfund, 10 Pfennig das Stück (*apiece, each*).
Er verdient 100 DM in der Woche, 400 DM im Monat, 5000 DM im Jahr. Er fuhr 80 Meilen in der Stunde.
Er kommt zweimal am Tage, in der Woche, im Monat. Er kommt zweimal die Woche.
Im Nu (*in a moment*); zum Spaß (*for a joke*); zur Abwechslung (*for a change*); im Trab/Galopp (*at a trot/gallop*); zur Not (*at a pinch*).

vi   Where English uses the possessive adjective, German the definite article:

Ich reichte ihm die (*my*) Hand. Er stand da, den Hut auf dem Kopf und die Hände in den Taschen.
Ich habe mich in die (*my*) Hand geschnitten. Er hat mir das Leben gerettet. Wasch dir die Hände!

13 The Gender of Nouns [1]

It is very often not possible to tell the gender of a noun from its meaning or form. The following rules, however, should be borne in mind:

(a) Generally speaking, nouns referring to males are masculine, to females, feminine, to their young (when the word exists), neuter, e.g. der Mann, die Frau, das Kind; der Stier, die Kuh, das Kalb; das Lamm, das Fohlen (*foal*); das Junge (*young of animals*).

[1] For the declension of nouns, see *101*

Note however the following exceptions:

der Backfisch (*flapper*), der Junge (*boy*), der Teenager.
die Ordonnanz (*orderly*), die Person, die Wache (*sentry*), die Waise (*orphan*).

das Frauenzimmer (*female*), das Fräulein, das Genie (*genius*), das Opfer (*victim*), das Weib (*woman, wife, derogatory now except in set phrases*, e.g. mit Weib und Kind), das Mädchen.

(b) Other parts of speech (except cardinal numerals) are nearly always neuter when used as nouns, e.g. das Schweigen, das Können, das Nichts, das Ja und Nein, das Für und Wider, das Auf und Ab, „Die Philosophie des Als Ob" (*title of book*).
But: die Fünf, die Sechs, unsere Elf.

(c) Suffixes usually indicating **masculine** nouns:
Native words: **-er** (*persons only*), **-ich, -ig, -ling, -s.**
Foreign words: **-ant, -ar** (*persons only*), **-är** (*persons only*), **-ast, -eur, -ier** (*persons only*), **-iker, -ismus, -ist, -loge, -or.**
Exception: **-ig**: das Reisig (*twigs*).

(d) Suffixes usually indicating **feminine** nouns:
Native words: **-e** (*not animate objects*), **-ei, -heit, -in** (*persons only*), **-keit, -schaft, -ung.**
Foreign words: **-ade, -age, -ance, -anz, -enz, -ette, -ie, -ik, -ille -ine, -ion, -isse, -itis, -ive, -ose, -sis, -tät, -ur, -üre.**
Exceptions: **-e**: der Buchstabe, Friede, Funke, Gedanke, Glaube, Haufe, Name, Wille, Käse, Kaffee, Tee.
das Auge, Ende, Erbe (*inheritance*), Knie, Gebäude, Gemüse.
Collectives in *Ge-* (mostly neuter, but see *15 1(e.)*)

(e) Suffixes usually indicating neuter nouns:
Native words: **-chen, -icht, -lein, -nis, -tel** (= -teil), **-tum.**
Foreign words: **-ett** (*not persons*), **-in** (*not persons*), **-ma, -ment, -um.**
Exceptions: **-icht**: der Habicht (*hawk*).
-nis: die Erlaubnis, Erkenntnis (*knowledge, realisation*), Finsternis, Verdamnis (*damnation*), Wildnis.
-tum: der Irrtum, der Reichtum.
-ment: der Moment (*moment*), der Zement.

(f) The nouns with the suffix **-sal** are sometimes feminine, sometimes neuter, sometimes both:
die Mühsal (*trouble*), Trübsal (*affliction*).
das Drangsal (*distress, also f.*), Scheusal (*monster*), Wirrsal (*confusion*).

14 Nouns whose Meaning Changes according to Gender

der Band (¨e)	*volume*	das Band (¨er)	*ribbon*
		das Band (-e)	*bond*
der Bord (-e)	*board (ship-)*	das Bord (-e)	*shelf*
der Bund (¨e)	*league,*	das Bund (-e)	*bundle, bunch (of*
	covenant		*keys)*
der Erbe (-n, -n)	*heir*	das Erbe (Erb-schaften)	*inheritance*
der Flur (-e)	*hall, vestibule*	die Flur (-en)	*meadow*
der Gefallen (-)	*favour*	das Gefallen[1]	*pleasure*
der Gehalt (-e)	*content*	das Gehalt (¨er)	*salary*
der Heide (-n, -n)	*heathen*	die Heide (-n)	*heather, moor*
der Hut (¨e)	*hat*	die Hut	*guard*
der Junge (-n, -n)	*boy*	das Junge (see 29)	*young of animals*
der Kiefer (-)	*jaw*	die Kiefer (-n)	*spruce fir*
der Kunde (-n, -n)	*customer*	die Kunde (-n)	*news, tidings*
der Leiter (-)	*manager*	die Leiter (-n)	*ladder*
das Mark	*marrow (of bone)*	die Mark (-en)	*marches*
		die Mark (-)	*mark (coin)*
der Messer (-)	*surveyor*	das Messer (-)	*knife*
der Moment (-e)	*moment*	das Moment (-e)	*motive, factor*
der Reis	*rice*	das Reis (-er)	*shoot, twig*
der Schild (-e)	*shield*	das Schild (-er)	*sign-board, label, name-plate*
der See (-n)	*lake*	die See	*sea*
das Steuer (-)	*rudder, helm, steering-wheel*	die Steuer (-n)	*tax*
der Tau	*dew*	das Tau (-e)	*rope*
der Taube (see 29)	*deaf man*	die Taube (-n)	*dove, pigeon*
der Tor (-en, -en)	*fool*	das Tor (-e)	*gate*
der Verdienst (-e)	*earnings*	das Verdienst (-e)	*merit, services*
das Wehr (-e)	*weir*	die Wehr (-en)	*defence, resistance*
der Weise (see 29)	*sage, wise man*	die Weise (-n)	*manner, way, melody, tune*

15 The Formation of Nouns

I Nouns can be formed by **derivation**

(a) From verbs:

  i By adding the masculine suffix **-er** to the stem or contracted stem of the infinitive, sometimes modifying the stem vowel, to denote agents, e.g. der Diener, Dichter, Maler, Heuchler (*hypocrite*), Käufer, Händler.

---

[1] Also masculine in this sense

ii By adding the feminine suffix **-ung** to the stem or contracted stem of the infinitive, e.g. die Dichtung, Handlung, Bedeutung, Einladung.

iii By the omission of the last letter of the infinitive (all feminine), e.g. die Rede, Ausrede (*excuse*), Regel, Klingel.

iv By adding the feminine suffix **-erei** to the stem of the infinitive (**-ei** if the stem ends in -*el* or -*er*), e.g. die Raserei (*frenzy*), Zauberei, Heuchelei.

v By substantivising the infinitive (all neuter), e.g. das Lesen, Versprechen, Lächeln.

(b) From adjectives or past participles:

i By adding **-e** to adjectives not ending in -*bar*, -*haft*, -*ig*, -*isch*, -*lich*, -*los* or -*sam* and modifying the vowel if possible (all feminine), e.g. die Ebene, Größe, Nähe, Wärme.

ii By adding the feminine suffixes **-heit, -schaft** to past pasticiples and to adjectives not ending in -*bar*, -*haft*, -*ig*, -*isch*, -*lich*, -*los* or -*sam*, e.g. die Schönheit, Vergangenheit, Eigenschaft, Gefangenschaft.

iii By adding the feminine suffix **-keit** to adjectives ending in -*bar*, -*ig*, -*lich* and -*sam*, e.g. die Dankbarkeit, Häufigkeit (*frequency*), Ähnlichkeit, Langsamkeit.

iv By adding the feminine suffix **-igkeit** to adjectives ending in -*haft* and -*los* and to a few others, e.g. die Mangelhaftigkeit, Machtlosigkeit, Müdigkeit, Kleinigkeit.

(c) From nouns or verbal nouns:

i By adding the feminine suffixes **-heit, -schaft**, e.g. die Christenheit (*Christendom*), Kindheit, Mannschaft, Leidenschaft.

ii By adding the feminine suffix **-ei**, e.g. die Bäckerei, Abtei (*abbey*, *abbacy*).

iii By adding the feminine suffix **-erei**, e.g. die Schurkerei, Schweinerei, die Kinderei.

iv By adding the neuter suffix **-tum**, (but see *13(e)*), e.g. das Christentum (*Christianity*), Judentum (*Jewry*).

(d) From nouns to form collectives by modification of the vowel usually and by adding the prefix **Ge-** and the suffix **-e** (the latter frequently omitted, especially after -*el* and -*er*), e.g. das Gelände, das Gebirge, das Gestirn, das Gemäuer.

(e) From verbs to form collectives as in (d) above, e.g. das Getriebe, das Gespräch. Often derogatory, e.g. das Getue, das Geplapper.

NOTE: Though most nouns beginning with *Ge-* are neuter there are a number of common exceptions, e.g.
(masculine): der Gedanke, Gebrauch, Gefallen (*favour*), Gehalt (*contents*), Geschmack, Genuß, Gesang, Gewinn
(feminine): die Gebärde (*gesture*), Gebühr (*fee*, *due*), Geburt, Geduld, Gefahr, Gemeinde (*congregation*), Geschichte, Gestalt

(f) From nouns by adding the particle **Un-** meaning (i) negation: das Unglück, die Ungeduld, die Unlust, der Unsinn, die Unruhe; (ii) 'a bad sort of': der Unmensch, die Unnatur, der Unstern, die Untat, das Untier; (iii) 'an excessive amount': die Unmenge, die Unsumme.

(g) From nouns by adding the particle **Ur-** meaning 'very old' or 'original': der Urvater, die Urwelt, der Urwald, die Ursprache, die Urform.

(h) From nouns to form diminutives (all neuter) by adding the suffixes **-chen** or **-lein** and usually modifying the vowel if possible, e.g. das Brötchen *roll*), das Fräulein. *But:* Frauchen (*little wife;* (*dog's, etc.*) *mistress*).

II The other method of noun formation is by **composition.** Note that:

(a) The gender and declension (see *101*) of a compound noun is always that of its last component: **der** Hausherr (-n, -en); **die** Kuhglocke (-n); **das** Flußufer (-); **die** Kiefernholzwand (≐e).

(b) Compounds consisting of two or more nouns are formed in the following ways:

i By simple juxtaposition of two or more nouns (forming so-called 'true' compounds), e.g. der Hausschlüssel, der Hauptstaat, das Fischerboot, der Lastautofahrer.

ii By adding **-s** or **-es** to the first noun (including feminine nouns!) before compounding. This is always done with *Armut* and with feminine nouns ending in *-heit, -keit, -schaft, -ung, -ion* and *-tät*; with masculine and neuter nouns ending in *-tum*; with infinitive-nouns; with strong masculine and neuter nouns that do not form 'true' compounds; and, generally, with nouns that are already compounded, e.g. die Sicherheitsnadel, der Wirklichkeitssinn, der Landschaftsmaler, die Überredungskunst, das Armutszeugnis (*certificate of poverty*), der Stationsvorsteher, der Universitätsprofessor; die Altertumskunde (*archaeology*); die Schaffenskraft; der Ortswechsel, die Geisteskraft, das Glückski 1; das Weihnachtslied, das Geburtstagsgeschenk.

iii By adding **-n** or **-en** to the first noun before compounding. This is normally done with feminine nouns that have none of the suffixes in (ii) above, as well as with masculine and neuter nouns of weak or mixed declension, e.g. der Ulmenast, der Sonnenschein; der Hirtenknabe, der Löwenanteil, der Augenblick.

iv By omitting the final **-e** of the first noun (nearly always feminine) before compounding, e.g. die Erdoberfläche.

v By simple juxtaposition, the first noun being plural, e.g. das Wörterbuch, die Bretterbude (*shanty*).

NOTE: Der Landmann (*farmer, countryman*), der Landsmann (*fellow-countryman, compatriot*); das Geschichtsbuch (*history book*), das Geschichtenbuch (*story-book*).

(c) Compounds are also formed consisting of a noun preceded by some other part of speech, e.g.

i   verb + noun: der Heizkörper, das Lesebuch, die Fahrkarte.

ii adjective or past participle + noun: die Hochzeit, der Gebraucht-wagen (*used car*).

iii numeral + noun: das Einhorn (*unicorn*), das Doppelsegel, die Erstge-burt, die Halbinsel (*peninsula*).

iv pronoun + noun: die Ichsucht (*selfishness*), die Selbstzucht (*self-discipline*).

v   preposition or adverb + noun: die Mehrzahl (*majority*), der Nebenfluß (*tributary*), der Rückweg, die Umwelt.

16 Nouns: Singular in German, Plural in English

(a) die Asche (*ashes*), die Brille (*spectacles*), der Dank, der Gram (*sorrows*), das Hauptquartier (*headquarters*), die Kaserne (*barracks*), der Lohn (*wages*), das Mittelalter (*Middle Ages*), die Schere (*scissors*), das Spielzeug (*toy(s)*), die Treppe (*stairs*), die Umgebung (*surroundings*); *and* die Ethik (*ethics*), die Physik, die Politik, die Statistik, etc.

(b) Some of these words have a plural, e.g. die Löhne, die Statistiken, die Brillen (*pairs of spectacles*), die Scheren (*pairs of scissors*), die Treppen (*flights of stairs*); er wohnt vier Treppen hoch (*on the fourth floor*).

17 Proper Nouns and Adjectives derived therefrom

(a) Afrika, Amerika, Asien, Australien, Europa; das Britische Weltreich; Ägypten, Belgien, Bulgarien, Celebes, China, Dänemark, England, Frankreich, Griechenland, Großbritannien (*UK* or *Great Britain*), Indien, Irland, Italien, Japan, Jugoslawien, Kanada, Litauen (*Lithuania*), Neuseeland, die Niederlande (*pl.*), Norwegen, Österreich, Polen, Portugal, Rumänien, Rußland, UdSSR (= *USSR*), Schottland, Schweden, die Schweiz, Spanien, die Tschechoslowakei, die Türkei, Ungarn, die Vereinigten Staaten (*USA*), Wales.

(b) Bayern (*Bavaria*), Brandenburg, das Elsaß, Hessen, Kärnten (*Carinthia*), Lothringen (*Lorraine*), Mittelengland (*the Midlands*), das Oberammergauerland, Ostpreußen, Pommern (*Pomerania*), Preußen, die Provence, das Rheinland, Sachsen, die Steiermark (*Styria*), Tirol, West-falen.

(c) Bern, Braunschweig (*Brunswick*), Brüssel, Florenz, Frankfurt am Main, Hannover, Lissabon, Luzern, Mandalay, Moskau, München, Nürnberg, Rom, Triest, Tripoli, Tschandrapur (*Chandrapore*), Venedig, Warschau.

(d) die Donau (*Danube*), die Elbe, die Isar, das Isartal, der Main, die Mosel, die Oder, der Rhein, die Seine, die Themse (*Thames*), die Weser; das Tote Meer; die/der Pont du Gard.

(e) der Afrikaner (-), der Amerikaner (-), der Araber (-), der Asiat (-en, -en), der Australier (-), der Bayer (-n, -n), der Bur (-en, -en) (*Boer*), der Belgier (-), der Chinese (-n, -n), der Däne (-n, -n), der Deutsche (*29*), der Engländer (-), der Franzose (-n, -n), der Grieche (-n, -n), der Holländer (-), der Inder (-), der Irländer (-) *or* Ire (-n, -n), der Italiener (-), der Japaner (-), der Kanadier (-), der Neuseeländer (-), der Norweger (-), der Österreicher (-), der Pole (-n, -n), der Portugiese (-n, -n), der Preuße (-n, -n), der Russe (-n, -n), der Sachse (-n, -n), der Schotte (-n, -n), der Schwede (-n, -n), der Spanier (-), der Südafrikaner (-), der Tscheche (-n, -n); der Türke (-n, -n), der Ungar (-n, -n), der Waliser (-).

(f) afrikanisch, amerikanisch, asiatisch, australisch, bayrisch, chinesisch, deutsch, englisch, eurasisch (*Eurasian*), europäisch, französisch, griechisch, holländisch, irisch, italienisch, kanadisch, polnisch, preußisch, römisch, russisch, walisisch, westindisch.

(g) Christus (*Christ*), der Jude (-n, -n), Kain, der Levit (-en, -en), der Samariter (*Samaritan*);
Königin Anne, Franz Josef (*Francis Joseph*), Johanna (*Joan*), Leibniz (*Leibnitz*), Königin Viktoria.

(h) die Aufklärung (*Enlightenment*), der Burenkrieg (*Boer War*), der Dreißigjährige Krieg, die Gegenreformation (*Counter Reformation*), der Siebenjährige Krieg, der Sturm und Drang, der Westfälische Friede (*Peace of Westphalia*), die Weimarer Klassik;
der Bolschewik/Bolschewist (-en, -en), der Faschist (-en, -en), die Habsburger (*pl.*), der Quäker (-), die Schwarz-Gelben (*Black and Tans*).

(i) bolschewistisch, elisabethanisch, habsburgisch, hegelsch (*Hegelian*), viktorianisch.

NOTE: The names of towns and of most countries are neuter.

18 The Declension of Proper Nouns

(a) Christian names (masculine and feminine) and surnames normally take -s in the genitive. If the name ends in s, ß, x, z, tz possession is shown by adding an apostrophe or by a preceding *von*.

> Karls Mutter, Elisabeths Schwester, Goethes Werke (*or* die Werke Goethes), Fritz' Hut (*or* der Hut von Fritz).

(b) With two or more names in combination only the last shows the genitive. With a surname including *von* if the name following *von* clearly refers to a place, only the last name preceding *von* shows the genitive ending.

Ricarda Huchs Romane; die Werke Friedrich von Schillers; unter der Regierung Friedrich Wilhelms des Zweiten von Preußen.

(c) If a title without article precedes a name, the name shows the genitive ending; if the title has the article, the title is inflected. *Herr* is always inflected in the oblique cases.

Onkel Herberts Wagen; der Wagen Onkel Herberts; der Wagen des Onkels Herbert; Professor Dr. Franks Sprechstunde; die Siege des Königs Friedrich des Zweiten; an Herrn Professor Lütgen.

(d) Surnames usually add -*s* to form the plural.

„Buddenbrooks". Wir gehen zu Schmidts. Das sind Dürers (*pictures by Dürer*).

(e) Place names are uninflected except in the masculine and neuter genitive and occasionally in the plural. When an article and adjective precedes, the genitive ending -*s* is now usually omitted.

Preußens Siege; die Erhebung Deutschlands; die Ufer des Rheins; die zwei Deutschland(s); des alten China.

(f) With geographical names ending in a sibilant possession is shown by *von* or by the addition of a preceding appositional noun.

die Landschaft von Wales; die Landschaft der Halbinsel Wales; die Theater der Hauptstadt Paris.

(g) The titles of books, plays, etc., remain unchanged if preceded by an appositional noun. If preceded by the author's name the article (if part of the title) is omitted; otherwise the full title is declined, leaving the article outside the inverted commas.

in dem Schauspiel „Die Räuber"; in Schillers „Räubern"; in den „Räubern".

(h) The months of the year are sometimes written with -*s* in the genitive, sometimes without. When preceded by a noun the months are uninflected. With the days of the week the genitive ending -*s* is still considered more correct.

die ersten Tage des August(s); Anfang Mai; Ende Juli; Mitte Juni; des Monats Mai; am Morgen des folgenden Montags.

19 The Nominative

The nominative is used to denote:

(a) The subject of the sentence: Der Tisch ist rund.

(b) The complement of the verbs *sein, bleiben, verbleiben, werden* and *heißen*: Ich bin und bleibe dein Freund. Er wurde mein zweiter Vater. Mit besten Grüßen verbleibe ich dein Freund. Er heißt Herr Schmidt.

20 The Accusative

The accusative is used:

(a) To denote the direct object of a transitive verb: Sie liebt ihren Vater.

(b) To denote duration of time and distance covered: Er blieb eine Weile, einen Monat (lang), einen Augenblick nur. Er ging einen Schritt weiter.

(c) To express measurements: Das Holz ist einen Finger dick/einen Zoll breit. Das Kind ist erst einen Monat alt. Sie sitzt drei Reihen weiter.

(d) In distributive expression (cf. *12(b)v*): Es kostet 3 Mark die Flasche/ das Stück/das Pfund.

(e) To denote 'definite time when' unless a preposition (*an, in*) is used: Er kommt nächsten Mittwoch, nächstes Jahr, jeden Tag; er kam voriges Jahr.

(f) To denote direction up or down: Er ging den Berg hinauf, die Treppe hinunter.

(g) In absolute constructions: Er saß da, den Kopf in die Hände gestützt.

(h) With certain adjectives: Ich bin/wurde ihn endlich los. Ich bin diese Arbeit gewohnt. Ich bin (*or* habe) diese Arbeit satt. Ich bin ihn überdrüssig (*sick of him*).

(i) In certain elliptic phrases: Vielen Dank! Guten Tag! Guten Abend! Herzliche Grüße! Herzliche Glückwünsche! (*Congratulations!*)

(j) After certain prepositions, see 52, 55.

21 The Genitive

The genitive is used:

(a) To denote possession: der Wagen meines Vaters; Goethes Werke.

NOTE: Except in the case of names and of close relatives, and in a few fixed phrases, a preceding genitive is now literary or archaic.

(b) To denote 'indefinite time when': Eines Tages (*one day*), eines schönen Apriltages, eines Abends, eines Nachts(!) verschwand er.

(c) To denote manner: Er fährt nur erster Klasse. Sei guten Mutes! Er sah mich unverwandten Blickes an. Wir gingen unseres Weges.

(d) With certain adjectives: bar (*devoid of*), bewußt (*aware of*), eingedenk (*mindful of*), entkleidet (*stripped of*), gewärtig (*prepared for*), gewiß (*certain of*), kundig (*thoroughly acquainted with*), ledig (*devoid, free of*), sicher (*sure of*), ungewohnt (*unused to*), unkundig (*ignorant of*), würdig (*worthy of*), e.g.

> Ich bin mir dessen bewußt. Er ist des Erfolgs sicher.

NOTE: Other adjectives like *fähig* (capable of), *müde, schuldig, überdrüssig, voll, wert* are also used with the genitive, but other constructions are possible, e.g. Er ist dieser Tat fähig; er ist zu allem fähig. Sie war voll weiblichen Charmes; der Saal war voll von (*or* mit) Menschen, war voll Menschen.

(e) In certain expressions: Ich bin der Meinung (*or* Ansicht). Es ist der Mühe wert. Es lohnt der (*or* die) Mühe (nicht). Wir sahen ihn dieser Tage (*the other day*). Sie wurde seiner ansichtig (*caught sight of him*). Sie werden auch der Segnungen der Zivilisation teilhaftig (*share in the blessings*). Die Stadt ist ihrer Vorrechte verlustig gegangen (*lost*).

(f) After certain prepositions, see *53*.

(g) After certain verbs, see *76, 77*.

22 The Dative

The dative is used:

(a) To denote the indirect object: Er gab mir das Buch.

(b) To denote interest or advantage: Kauf mir ein Buch! Ich habe mir eine Zigarette angezündet (*lit myself a ...*).

(c) To denote possession (restricted almost exclusively to parts of the body): Es flog ihm ins Gesicht (*into his face*). Er rettete mir das Leben (*my*).

(d) With certain adjectives, which tend mostly to follow the noun or pronoun they govern: abhold (*averse from/to*), abgeneigt (*averse from/to*), ähnlich (*similar to, like*), (un)begreiflich (*(in)comprehensible to*), (un)bekannt, dankbar, ebenbürtig (*equal to, rivalling*), eigen (*peculiar to*), ergeben (*devoted to*), fern, fremd (*alien to*), gemäß (*appropriate, conformable(y) to*), gemeinsam (*common to*), gewachsen (*a match for, up to*), gleich (*like, the same for*), gleichgültig, langweilig, lästig (*a nuisance to*), nachteilig, nahe, am nächsten (*nearest to*), nützlich, schädlich, (un)sympathisch ((*un*)*congenial to*), treu (*loyal to*), überlegen (*superior to*), untergeordnet (*subordinate to*), unterworfen (*subject to*), (un)verständlich, ((*in*)*comprehensible to*), vertraut (*familiar to*), zuwider (*repugnant to*), e.g.

> Er ist seiner Mutter ganz ähnlich. Er ist jeder Arbeit abgeneigt. Er ist ihm nicht gewachsen. Dieser Instinkt ist allen Menschen gemeinsam. Er ist mir sympathisch (*I like him*). Das ist mir gleich.

(e) In certain idiomatic phrases: Das Kleid ist mir zu lang. Mir ist zu kalt, mir ist warm. Mir ist schlecht/gut/wohl zumute. Er tat es mir zuliebe (*for my sake*). Ich stehe ihm zu Diensten (*at his service*). Das gereicht ihm zur Ehre (*does him honour*). Das kam ihm zugute (*was for his advantage*). Das wurde mir zuteil (*allotted to*). Wie dem auch sei (*however that may be*); dem ist so (*that is the case*); wenn dem so ist (*if that is so*). Ich stelle dir den Wagen zur Verfügung (*I place my car at your disposal*). Der Wagen steht dir zur Verfügung (*is at your disposal*). Es steht uns frei, zu. . . (*we are free to . . .*). Das Buch ist mir abhanden gekommen (*I have lost*).

(f) After certain prepositions, see 54, 55.

(g) After certain verbs, see 74, 75.

23 Apposition

(a) The noun in apposition is normally in the same case as the noun or pronoun with which it stands in apposition. Note:

  i Mein Lehrer, ein großer Gelehrter; von ihm, einem großen Gelehrten, hätte ich das nicht erwartet; der Nachfolger Wilhelms des Eroberers; ein Paar Handschuhe; am Freitag, dem (*or* den) 17. April; die Universität Göttingen (*of G.*); die Hochhäuser der Stadt Berlin; in der Stadt Berlin; im Monat Mai.

 ii Ein Dutzend Eier; mit einem Dutzend Eiern; der Preis einer Flasche Rotweins. *But:* der Preis eines Stückes Rindfleisch (*to avoid double strong genitive*).

iii Ein Paar schwarze (*or* schwarzer (G.)) Schuhe; mit einem Dutzend frischen Eiern (*or* frischer Eier (G.)).

(b) Note the similar construction after **als** (*as, as a*) and **wie** (*like*):

  i Ich als ältester Sohn; mir als jüngstem Bruder; die Kunst als solche; Tolstois Beschimpfung der Ärzte als nichtsnutziger Schufte (T. MANN). Ich kenne mich aus mit Menschen wie Ihnen (ANDERSCH).

 ii Er wurde als ehrenhafter Mann betrachtet. Sie erkannte ihn als ihren Sohn wieder. Er sieht wie ein ganz gesunder Mensch aus.

But Er betrachtet sich als großer Dichter (*accusative now obsolete*).

24 The Formation of Adjectives

(a) A large number of adjectives are formed by means of the following suffixes and prefixes:

i From nouns by adding the adjective-suffixes **-reich** (*rich in*), **-voll** (*full of*), **-los** (*lacking in*), **-wert** and **-würdig** (*-worthy*), **-fertig** (*ready to*), **-dicht** (*proof against*), **-fest** (*resisting, firm as*), **-sicher** (*safe against*), **-frei** (*free of*), **-artig** (*resembling*), **-mäßig** (*like*):

aufschlußreich (*revealing*), hoffnungsreich, kinderreich; liebevoll sorgenvoll; erfolglos, hoffnungslos, kinderlos; lesenswert, lobenswert, liebenswürdig; reisefertig; wasserdicht; feuerfest, felsenfest; bombensicher; zollfrei; eigenartig; regelmäßig

ii From nouns by adding the suffixes **-ig** (= *1. possession; 2. nature; 3. similarity*), **-isch** (= *1. origin* (*derived from proper names*); *2. qualities* (*mostly bad*); *3. -ic and -ical*) and **-(e)n** or **-ern** (= *made of*):

geduldig, sandig, silberig, jetzig; russisch, Kölnisch Wasser; kindisch; historisch, musikalisch; seiden, bleiern, steinern

iii From nouns, adjectives and verbs by adding the suffix **-lich** or **-erlich** (= *1. similarity; 2. possession; 3. approximation*):

kindlich, männlich, herzlich, täglich, rötlich, kränklich, fraglich, zerbrechlich, unbeschreiblich; lächerlich, fürchterlich

iv From nouns of towns by adding the suffix **-er**. Such adjectives are written with a capital and do not inflect.

im Kölner Dom; die Münchener Zeitungen

v From adjectives, verb-stems or nouns by adding the suffix **-bar** (= *1. bearing; 2. -able, -ible*), **-haft** (= *1. subject to; 2. characteristic of*) and **-sam** (= *capacity or tendency*):

fruchtbar, offenbar, eßbar, unverkennbar; krankhaft, nahrhaft, mädchenhaft; langsam, sparsam, friedsam

vi From adjectives by adding the prefixes **un-** (= *in-, im-, dis-, un-*) and **ur-** (= *very*):

unmenschlich, unmöglich, unzufrieden, ungesund; uralt, urplötzlich

(b) Foreign suffixes are numerous but are only very rarely used with native words:

rent*abel*, nation*al*, hum*an*, mond*än*, risk*ant*, interstell*ar*, revolution*är*, priv*at*, tradition*ell*, intellig*ent*, grot*esk*, kompl*ett*, flex*ibel*, hybr*id*, stab*il*, mass*iv*, dubi*os*, nerv*ös*

(c) Compound adjectives are formed by the juxtaposition of (i) two adjectives: *hellblau, dunkelrot*; (ii) of noun and adjective: *aschblond, schneeweiß, zimmerrein*; (iii) of numeral or numeral pronoun and adjective or adjectival

suffix: *dreieckig, vierstöckig, mehrstöckig, zweistündig, dreitägig, vierjährig*;
(iv) of adverb or noun and present participle: *vielversprechend, weitreichend, atemberaubend haarsträubend*.

(d) Note the following compound (intensified) adjectives which are the equivalent of similes:

blitzschnell, federleicht, hellwach, lammfromm, mäuschenstill, mausetot, pechdunkel, rabenschwarz, saugrob, schnurgerade, steinhart, steinreich (*enormously rich*), stockdürr, stocktaub, todmüde

25 The Predicative Adjective

(a) The adjective used predicatively, i.e. after the verbs *sein, werden, bleiben, scheinen* has no case or gender inflection.

Er ist alt. Sie wird immer jünger. Er scheint jünger, als er ist. Bleib gesund!

(b) A small number of adjectives are used only predicatively, of which the most common are: allein, barfuß, gar (*properly cooked, done*), quitt (*quits*), schuld (*to blame*), unpaß (*unwell*); gang und gäbe (*customary*).

26 The Attributive Adjective

(a) See *91–93* for paradigms of declension.

(b) Note the following points:

i The attributive adjective is declined weak (see *86(b)*) when preceded by the definite article or any word similarly declined strong. Otherwise the adjective is declined strong (see *93*).

ii Two or more ordinary attributive adjectives preceding the noun have each the same inflection (but see *28(c)*).

iii The inflection of the possessive adjective (see *89*) immediately following *all(er), dieser, jener* is unaffected by them:

mit all(er) **meiner** Kraft; mit diesem **meinem** Wort; all(e) **meine** Freunde.

iv The inflection of *dieser* and *jener* immediately following *all(er)* is unaffected by it:

die Straßen all(er) **dieser** Städte.

v The adjective after the personal pronoun should by the rule given above ((*b*)*i*) be declined strong. In the feminine dative singular and nominative plural however it is now usually declined weak (cf. *37(p)iv*):

ich armer Mann, ihm altem/alten Mann, uns Deutsche (*acc.*); *but* ihr armen Frau, wir/ihr Deutschen, wir armen Leute.

vi After the genitive of the relative pronoun and of *zwei, drei* the adjective is declined strong.

die Mutter, deren ältester Sohn ...; der Mann, mit dessen ältestem Sohn ...
die Freundschaft zweier/dreier großer Völker.

27 Indeclinable Adjectives

(a) Adjectives ending in -*er* derived from the names of towns (see *24(a)iv*)

(b) A few adjectives of foreign origin denoting colours, e.g. *beige, creme, lila, oliv, orange, rosa* (often inflected, however, in conversation), and the words *prima* (first rate) and *uni* (plain, of one colour):

ein **rosa**/rosa(n)es Band, ein **orange**/orangenes Kleid; **prima** Tee
But ein rosafarbiges/rosafarbenes Kleid, ein olivgrüner Rock

28 Uninflected Adjectives

(a) Adjectives in apposition following or preceding a noun or pronoun:

Ein Edelmann ganz und gar auch er, **unabhängig** und **stolz**... (E. MARCKS)
Vulkanisch und **gütig** und im Innersten **fromm**, er steht unter ihnen... (E. MARCKS)

(b) In a very few stereotyped expressions, e.g. auf **gut** Glück, ein **halb** Dutzend, ein **gut** Stück des Weges; sie sind wieder **gut** Freund.

(c) The first of two attributive colour adjectives, e.g. viele **weiß** und schwarze Kühe.

(d) In poetry and in proverbial expressions, before neuter singular nouns and after nouns of any gender or number:

Unrecht Gut gedeiht nicht. (*Ill-gotten gains seldom prosper*).
Röslein **rot**. O Täler **weit**!

29 The Adjective-Noun

(a) Adjective-nouns can refer to persons or to things and are usually written with a capital.

der Kranke; die Kranke; die Kranken (*pl.*); das Schöne, das Innere (*interior*); das Böse (*evil*).

(b) They are declined for the most part according to the usual rules applying to adjectives (see *91–93*):

ein Kranker; mit dem Kranken; einige Kranke; Junge und Alte; des Schönen. *But:* dir als gut**em** Bekannt**en**.

(c) Certain former noun-adjectives have now become weak nouns (see *101*), e.g. der Junge (*boy*), (*but not* das Junge (*young of animals*)), der Invalide (*disabled soldier*).

(d) After *etwas, viel, soviel, wenig, nichts* and *allerlei* the adjective-noun is declined strong.

Nom., *acc.* etwas Gutes; *gen.* (*rare*) etwas Guten; *dat.* etwas Gutem.

(e) After *alles, vieles, weniges* the adjective-noun is declined weak.

Nom., *acc.* alles Gute; *gen.* alles Guten; *dat.* allem Guten.

NOTE: Certain adjectives in (a), (d) and (e) above are written with small letters, e.g. etwas anderes, alles mögliche alles übrige, das einzige.

(f) The neuter adjective-noun is widely used in German and will often be found to offer a neat translation of abstract nouns preceded by the indefinite article, or of English expressions involving such words as 'thing(s)', 'course', 'quality', 'phenomenon', 'element(s)', 'touch', 'what is', 'much that is'.

etwas Bezauberndes (*a fascination*), das erste (*the first thing*), das einzige (*the only thing*), das Allernötigste (*the very most necessary thing*), viel Liebes (*lots of nice things*), das Verrückte daran (*the crazy thing about it*), Wichtiges und Wertvolles (*things/lessons of importance and value*), das Sicherste (*the safest course*), das Wahnsinnige (*the frantic quality/mad thing*), das Auffallendste (*the most striking phenomenon*), etwas Katzenartiges (*a feline element*), das Gegensätzliche (*conflicting elements*), das Gedachte und Gesagte (*what is thought and said*), viel Dramatisches (*much that is dramatic*).

30 Adjectives in Titles

Such adjectives are attributive although they follow the noun. They are declined weak and are written with a capital.

Friedrichs des Großen; Elisabeths der Zweiten

31 The Comparison of Adjectives

(a) Predicative:

Der Fluß ist breit, breiter, hier am breitesten.

(b) Attributive:

Das ist ein breiter, ein breiterer, der breiteste Fluß.

NOTE: Most adjectives of one syllable modify the vowels **a, o** or **u** (but not **au**) in the comparative and superlative. Common exceptions are: bunt, falsch, flach, froh, hohl, kahl, klar, rasch, rund, satt, stumpf (*blunt*), voll, wahr. None of these modify.

(c) Irregular forms of comparison:

groß	größer	am größten/der größte
gut	besser	am besten/der beste
hoch	höher	am höchsten/der höchste
nah	näher	am nächsten/der nächste
viel	mehr[1]	am meisten/das meiste
wenig	{ weniger[1]	am wenigsten/das wenigste
	minder	am mindesten/das mindeste

(d) Examples of comparison of adjectives:

i Er ist (eben) so alt, nicht so alt, bei weitem nicht so alt wie ich. Es ist ebenso gefährlich wie kostbar. Wir sind gleich alt (*both the same age*).

ii Er ist reicher, viel reicher, noch (*even*) reicher, bei weitem reicher, weniger reich als ich.
Er wird immer reicher (*richer and richer*). Er ist mehr fleißig als klug.
Er ist nichts weniger als klug (*anything but clever*).
Mehr oder minder gut. Um so (*or* desto) besser.
Es ist um so wichtiger, als ... (*all/so much the more ... because*).

iii Ein älterer (*elderly*) Herr; ein längerer (*prolonged*) Aufenthalt; die neuere (*modern*) Geschichte.
Helga und Irma sehen sich ähnlich, doch hat erstere (*the former*) schwarze, letztere (*the latter*) blonde Haare.
Es wäre besser, wenn wir jetzt gingen (*we had better go now*).

iv Er ist der klügste von allen. Das ist das schönste aller Kleider/von, unter allen Kleidern. Er ist mit der klügste (*one of the cleverest*) in der Klasse.
Das allerbeste; die weitaus gebildetsten (*by far the most cultured*).
Die meiste Zeit, die meisten Leute, die meisten von uns.
Es ist am besten, wenn wir gehen. Es wäre das beste, nichts zu sagen.
Ich halte es für das beste, du schweigst.

32 The Formation of Adverbs

(a) The predicative adjective and the past and present participle may generally be used as an adverb:

Er arbeitet fleißig. Er kam unerwartet/überraschend schnell.

[1] Indeclinable

(b) Some adverbs are formed from other parts of speech by adding such suffixes as: **-erweise**, **-weise**, **-s**, **-lich**, (bekanntlich), **-lings** (blindlings), **-wärts** (heimwärts), **-e** (lange), **-(e)ns** (namens, höchstens), **-maßen**, **-heim** (daheim), **-halber** (gesundheitshalber).

(c) Some adverbs are underived words like: hier, dort, da, dann, irgend, nie, je, etc.

33 Adverbs of Manner

NOTE:
(a) The very common suffix **-weise** (= -*wise*, (*bit*) *by* (*bit*), *by way of*) added to nouns: stückweise, teilweise, schrittweise, beispielsweise, ausnahmsweise, bissenweise (*in mouthfuls*).

(b) The common suffix **-erweise** (= *it is . . . ly the case that, . . .ly enough*) changes the meaning of an existing adverb:

Sie ist erstaunlich jung. Erstaunlicherweise wußte er nichts davon.

(c) The suffix **-maßen** (= *in . . . measure, to . . . extent*) added to the genitive plural of adjectives and pronouns:

einigermaßen, gewissermaßen, unverdientermaßen.

(d) The common modal adverbs:

anders (*different*), fast/beinahe (*almost*), eigentlich (*strictly speaking, actually, as a matter of fact*), ungefähr/etwa (*approximately*), leider (*unfortunately*), natürlich (*of course*), sogar/selbst (*even*), umsonst/vergebens (*in vain*), vielleicht, ziemlich (*rather*), zufällig (*by chance*).

34 Adverbs of Time

NOTE:
(a) Adverbs formed by the suffix **-s** to mean 'of a (morning)', 'during the (morning)', 'every (morning)': morgens, vormittags, mittags, nachmittags, abends, nachts, sonntags, wochentags, winters, etc.

(b) Adverbs formed by the suffix **-lang** added to the plural of nouns to mean 'for . . .', 'for . . . on end': sekundenlang, minutenlang, stundenlang, tagelang, wochenlang, monatelang, jahrelang, jahrhundertelang.

(c) The adverbial use of **lang** in time phrases like: einen Augenblick lang ((*for*) *a moment*), mehrere Tage lang, etc.

(d) Immer wieder (*again and again*).

35 Adverbs of Place

(a) Place where (**wo?**): da, dort, hier, draußen (*out(-side)*), drinnen (*inside, within*), oben (*at the/on top*), unten (*at the bottom*), vorn, hinten, rechts, **links**, drüben (*over there*), überall, irgendwo, nirgendwo/nirgends, woanders/anderswo, unterwegs (*on the way*).

(b) Place where to (**wohin?**): dahin, dorthin, hierhin, hinaus, hinein, hinauf/nach oben, hinunter/nach unten, nach vorn, nach hinten, nach rechts, nach links, nach drüben, überallhin, irgendwohin, nirgendwohin, anderswohin.

(c) Place from where (**woher?**): daher/von da, hierher/von hier, von dort, von draußen, von drinnen, von oben, von unten, von vorn, von hinten, von rechts, von links, von drüben, (von) überallher, (von) irgendwoher, (von) nirgendwoher, (von) anderswoher.

(d) Motion away from the speaker = **hin**; towards the speaker = **her**. Therefore:

Ich gehe hin, hinaus, hinein, hinauf, hinunter, hinab, hinan, hinüber.
Er kommt her, heraus, herein, herauf, herunter, herab, heran, herüber.
Ich ging den Berg/die Treppe hinauf.
Er kam den Berg/die Treppe herunter.

(e) Note the double forms (i) two adverbs; (ii) preposition + adverb; (iii) adverbial compound + adverb:

i Er ging **auf** und **ab** (*up and down*), **hin** und **her** (*hither and thither, to and fro, this way and that*). Wir gehen **ab** und **zu/hin** und **wieder/ dann** und **wann** (*now and again*) ins Kino.

ii Er ging **am** Fluß **entlang** (*along*), **am** Dom **vorbei** (*past*), **auf** sie **zu** (*up to, towards*), **durch** die Lücke **hindurch** (*through the gap*), **hinter/neben/vor** ihr **her** (*along behind/next/in front of her*), **ins** Dorf **hinab/hinunter** (*down into*), **in** das Zimmer **hinein** (*into*), **nach** dem Wald **zu** (*towards*). Er kam **zu** mir **herüber** (*across*). Er sah **nach/zu** mir **hin** (*towards me, in my direction*), **vor** sich **hin** (*straight in front*); es kam **von oben/unten her** (*from above/below*); sie standen **um** mich **her/herum** (*round about me*). Es läuft **auf** dasselbe **hinaus** (*amounts to the same thing*); die Fenster gehen **nach** dem Garten **hinaus** (*look out on to*); er wohnt **nach hinten hinaus** (*at the back*); das Zimmer **nach hinten hinaus** (*the back room*); er sah **zum** Fenster **hinaus/heraus** (*out of*); das Wasser floß **über** die Steine **hinweg** (*flowed over*). **Auf** die Gefahr **hin** (*at the risk*), **auf** meinen Rat **hin** (*on my advice*); **aus** einer natürlichen Abneigung **heraus** (*from*), **aus** unserem eigenen Empfinden **heraus, aus** dem Verlangen **heraus**; **nach außen hin**

(*outwardly*), **nach oben hin** (*towards the top*); **über** das Ziel **hinaus**
(*beyond*), **über** den Tod **hinaus** (*after*); **aus** der Erde **hervor**
(*from under*); **von** dem Tage **an** (*from that day onwards*), **von** Anfang
an; **von** klein **an/auf** (*from childhood*); **von** dort **aus, vom** Fenster
aus, von Natur **aus** (*by nature*), **von** mir **aus** (*as far as I am concerned*).

iii Er sah nicht weiter **darüber hinaus** (*beyond it, further*); das Wasser
floß **darüber hinweg** (*over it*); er geht **darüber hinweg** (*ignores,
disregards it*); er kommt **darüber hinweg** (*gets over it*); er sieht **darüber
hinweg** (*overlooks it*).

36 The Comparison of Adverbs

(a) Adverbs have the same comparison as predicative adjectives (*31(a)*).
Note however the following irregularities:

bald	eher/früher	am ehesten/am frühesten
gern	lieber	am liebsten
gut/wohl	besser	am besten
viel/sehr	mehr	am meisten
wenig	weniger/minder	am wenigsten/am mindesten

Komm so schnell du kannst (*as quickly as you can*)!

Er stürzte hinaus, so schnell er konnte (*as fast as he could*).

Er verdient weniger als ich. Dieser Zug fährt am schnellsten.

Sie fahren am besten mit dem Frühzug.

Er sorgt für mich mehr als Koch denn als Vater (*as ... than*).

(b) Adverbs have in addition an absolute superlative: aufs wärmste, aufs
beste, aufs schönste, etc.

Compare: Er begrüßte sie **am herzlichsten** (*most cordially*, i.e. *more
cordially than the others, than on other occasions*).

Er begrüßte sie **aufs herzlichste** (*most*, i.e. *exceedingly cordially*).

(c) Note the following forms of the superlative:

i erstens, letztens (*in the first, last place*); frühestens, höchstens,
spätestens (*at the earliest, most, latest*); meist/meistens (*mostly*)
strengstens (*strictly*); wenigstens/mindestens (*at least*); nicht im min-
desten (*not in the least*); nicht zum wenigsten/mindesten im Sommer
(*not least in summer*); nächster Tage (*in the course of the next few days*);
nächstens/demnächst (*shortly, in the near future*).
Wollen Sie gütigst Platz nehmen (*please be seated*)! Es geht ihm bestens
(*very well*). Ich lasse ihm bestens danken (*send him my best thanks*).

ii höchst (*most*) dumm; äußerst (*extremely*) klug; das meist aufgeführte
Stück (*the most performed play*).
Komm möglichst schnell (*as quickly as possible*)!

37 Cardinal Numbers

Note the following points of spelling and usage:

(a) Sechzehn, siebzehn, sechzig, siebzig, hundert (*one hundred*), tausend; (im Jahre) neunzehnhundertvierundsechzig (*in 1964*).

(b) Eins (*when not followed by its dependent noun*), hunderteins, hundertzwei, tausendeins; einmal eins ist eins; eins Komma null sechs (= *1·06*); zehn nach eins (=zehn Minuten nach ein Uhr).

(c) Um ein Uhr, vor ein oder zwei Tagen, mit ein wenig/bißchen Geduld, mit ein paar Freunden, von hundertein Städten (*or* von hundertundeiner Stadt), in ein und derselben Straße, er ist mein ein und alles.

(d) Der Mann, dessen einer Sohn/eines Kind (*whose one ...*); diese eine Frau, sein eines Glas Wasser.

(e) Noch ein (*another*) Brötchen, noch zwei Glas Bier.

(f) In telephoning *zwo* is used for *zwei*: zwo acht—sieben sechs—null drei (287603).

(g) Die Freundschaft zweier/dreier großer Völker; er ging auf allen vieren; wir sind/gehen/sitzen zu zweien/zu zweit, zu dreien/zu dritt, zu vieren/zu viert. (Zu vieren = *in groups of four*; zu viert = *four in a group*.)

(h) Die Null, die Eins, die Zwei etc. (= *the figures 0, 1, 2, etc.*).

(i) Er bekam eine Eins, eine Vier (*or* einen Einser, einen Vierer) (= *school marks or gradings*); die Elf gewann das Spiel (mit) acht zu vier.

(j) Wir fahren mit der Fünfzehn (= *tram or bus*).

(k) Er ist ein Mann Mitte Fünfzig, über Fünfzig, um die mittleren Vierzig, in den Fünfzigern (*in his fifties*).

(l) Es geschah in den zwanziger/dreißiger Jahren (*in the 'twenties/'thirties*).

(m) Ein Achter (*a rowing 'eight'*); ein Achtziger/eine Achtzigerin (*octogenarian*). Ich habe nur einen Zwanziger/Hunderter (= *20/100 mark note*). Er ist in den Achtzigern (*in his eighties*).

(n) Hunderte/Tausende von Menschen; Tausende und Abertausende (*thousands and thousands*); einige Hunderte/Tausende; zu Hunderten und Tausenden; einige hundert/tausend Menschen (*a few hundred/thousand*); ein paar hundert/tausend Schritt(e).

(o) Zwei Dutzend Eier, ein halbes Dutzend Nägel.

(p) Beid- (*both, the two*)

i Beide Brüder, die beiden Brüder, meine beiden Brüder.

ii Keine der beiden Parteien (*neither of the (two) parties*); ich mag beide nicht (*I don't like either of them = persons*).

iii Die ersten beiden (= *the first and second*); die beiden ersten (= *the two who are first*).

iv Wir beide, ihr beide, sie beide; wir beiden Deutschen; ihr beiden andern (*you other two*). Wir kamen beide früh an.

v Beides (= *either of two things*) ist möglich. Ich mag beides nicht. Keines von beidem (*neither*).

38 Ordinal Numbers

Note the following points of spelling and usage:

(a) Der erste, der dritte, der sieb(en)te, der achte.

(b) Das erste beste Hotel (= *the first hotel* (*you come to*)); der zweitbeste, der drittbeste Roman; der vorletzte/zweitletzte (*last but one*), der drittletzte; der zweithöchste, der dritthöchste.

(c) Erstklassig, zweitklassig; erstrangig, zweitrangig.

(d) Er war der erste, der das sagte (*the first to say that*).

(e) Das erstemal, zum erstenmal; das erste Mal, zum ersten Mal.

(f) Der erste April, den zweiten Mai, am dritten Juni; der Erste des Monats.

(g) Er ist der Erste der Klasse; er kam als erster an (*was the first to arrive*).

(h) Friedrich der Zweite, Ludwig der Vierzehnte, Erste Hilfe.

39 Fractions

(a) (ein) halb, in halb Europa, eine halbe Stunde, das halbe Jahr, ein halbes Dutzend, auf halbem (Wege (*half way*), alle halbe Stunde (*every half hour*); die Hälfte meines Vermögens (*half my fortune*); wir kennen ihn nur zur Hälfte.

(b) eineinhalb/anderthalb Stunden ($1\frac{1}{2}$ hours), zweieinhalb, dreieinhalb, etc. (The forms *dritt(e)halb* ($2\frac{1}{2}$), *viert(e)halb* ($3\frac{1}{2}$), etc., are now obsolete.)

(c) ein Drittel, ein Viertel, das Sechstel meines Vermögens; zwei Drittel, sieben Zwanzigstel, ein Hundertstel, drei Hunderteintel, drei Hundertzweitel etc.

(d) eine Viertelstunde, zwei Viertelstunden, in (einer) dreiviertel Stunde (*or* in drei viertel Stunden) (= *45 minutes*) ein, drei achtel Liter, eine hundertstel Sekunde.

40 Other Numeral Expressions

(a) einmal (*once*), zweimal, dreimal, etc.; vier mal vier ist sechzehn; kein einziges Mal (*not once*); nicht einmal (*not even!*).

(b) einfach (*simple*), zweifach (*twofold*), dreifach, etc.; mehrfach, vielfach, mannigfach/mannigfaltig (*manifold*); einfältig (*simple-minded!*).

(c) doppelt (*double*), ein doppeltes Vergnügen, doppelt so groß wie; um das Doppelte größer.

(d) einerlei (*of one kind*), zweierlei, dreierlei, etc.; zweierlei Arbeit; Sagen und Tun sind zweierlei (*two different things*); Kinder beiderlei Geschlechts; keinerlei Unterschied (*no distinction of any kind*); vielerlei Leute, allerlei Bücher; mir war das ganz einerlei (*all the same*).

(e) einzig (*sole, only, single, solitary*), sein einziges Kind, eine einzige Ausnahme, das einzige, was ... (*the only thing that*); einzigartig (*unique*).

(f) einzeln (*separate(ly), singly, individual*), sie kamen einzeln an, die Bände werden einzeln (*singly*) verkauft; ins einzelne gehen (*go into details*), der Einzelne (*the individual*) ist machtlos; vereinzelt (= *occasional*).

(g) einsam (*lonely*), eine einsame Straße.

(h) erstens (*first, in the first place*), zweitens, drittens ... letztens.

41 Measurements

Masculine and neuter nouns denoting measurements do not inflect in the plural; feminine nouns, however, (except *Mark*) do inflect in the plural.

10 Pfund, 4 Fuß breit, 100 Schritt (*100 yards*), 6 Meter zu (*by*) 3 Meter, 2000 m hoch. 8 Meter im Quadrat (*8 metres square*), 20 Quadratmeter groß (*20 square metres in size*), drei Paar Strümpfe, mit drei Paar Strümpfen; sie bekamen je (*they each got*) 20 Mark. *But* zwei Tassen Tee, drei Flaschen Rotwein, drei Meilen.

37

42 Time

(a) By the clock:

i   Wieviel Uhr ist es? Wie spät ist es?
    Es ist ein Uhr/eins, fünf (Minuten) nach eins/ein Uhr fünf, Viertel
    nach eins/Viertel zwei, halb zwei, Viertel vor zwei/dreiviertel zwei,
    zehn (Minuten) vor zwei.
    Es ist zwölf Uhr, es ist Mittag, Mitternacht, es ist halb zwölf.
    Es ist 3 Uhr nachts, 6 Uhr morgens, 10 Uhr vormittags, 3 Uhr
    nachmittags, 6 Uhr abends, 11 Uhr nachts.
ii Um (*at*) wieviel Uhr? Um 7 Uhr, gegen (*about*) 8 Uhr, um (*round
    about*) Mittag/Mitternacht. Ich komme Punkt 5 Uhr an.
iii Die Uhr geht vor, geht nach, geht richtig.
iv Es ist ein Uhr (*it is one o'clock*); es ist eine Uhr (*it is a clock*); eine
    Stunde (*an, one hour, a lesson*).

(b) Date and age

i   Der wievielte ist heute? Heute ist der zweite April.
ii Wann kommt er? Er kommt nächsten Mittwoch, nächste Woche,
    nächstes Jahr, in den nächsten Tagen, nächster Tage, Dienstag,
    Dienstag abend, am Mittwoch, am Sonntagmorgen, am Montag-
    abend, am zweiten April, im September; er kommt am Freitag, dem/
    den 18. Februar.
    Wann war die Schlacht bei Belle Alliance (*what was the date of the
    battle of Waterloo?*)?
    Wann bist du geboren? Ich bin/wurde (=*formal*) (im Jahre) 1950
    geboren. Wann wurde Goethe geboren? Er wurde (im Jahre) 1749
    geboren (wurde . . . geboren *used of deceased persons*). Er war damals
    noch nicht geboren (worden) (*had not yet been born*).
iii Er ist sechs (Jahre alt); mit sechs Jahren ging ich zur Schule (*at the
    age of 6*). In reiferen Jahren (*at a riper age*) denkt man anders. Er ist
    in den besten Jahren (*in his prime*). Er ist schon bei Jahren (*getting on in
    years*). Im Jahre 1 000 vor Christi Geburt (*B.C.*), nach Christi Geburt
    (*A.D.*).
iv Er steht in meinem Alter (*is my age*), im besten Mannesalter (*in the
    prime of life*). Er starb im Alter von 60 Jahren. In ihrem Alter (*at her
    age*) war ich viel größer. Er ist ein Mann mittleren Alters (*middle-
    aged*), in mittlerem Alter (*in middle life*).

NOTE: Im Mittelalter (= *in the Middle Ages*); mittelalterlich (= *medieval*).

v   Weihnachten/Ostern/Pfingsten (*Christmas/Easter/Whitsun*) kommt
    bald. Wir wünschen Ihnen fröhliche Weihnachten/Ostern, ein
    fröhliches Weihnachtsfest, ein gesegnetes Osterfest. Er kam zu
    Weihnachten/Silvester (*New Year's Eve*)/Neujahr/Ostern/Pfingsten/zu
    den Ferien (*for the holidays*) nach Hause. Er kommt am Weihnachts-

38

abend (*Christmas Eve*) am ersten Weihnachtstag (*Christmas Day*) am zweiten Weihnachtstag (*Boxing Day*).

(c) Idiomatic expressions of time

i   heute abend (*tonight, i.e. before bed-time*), heute nacht/diese Nacht (*tonight, i.e. after bed-time; last night, i.e. during the night*), morgen früh (*tomorrow morning*), gestern abend (*last night*), vorgestern, übermorgen.

ii acht Tage (*a week*), vierzehn Tage (*fortnight*), vor acht Tagen, heute vor acht Tagen (*a week ago today*), in vierzehn Tagen (*in a fortnight's time*), morgen in 14 Tagen/über 14 Tage.

iii Er kam am Morgen, am Abend, am vorigen Abend, am Vorabend (*eve*) der Hochzeit, am andern Tag (*the following day*), am nächsten Morgen, voriges Jahr, in einem anderen Jahr (*another year*), in der vorigen Woche, vorigen/letzten Dienstag. An **dem** Abend (*that night*).

43 Personal Pronouns

(a) See *98* for declension.

(b) *Du* (sing.) and *ihr* (pl.) are the familiar forms of address used with relatives, close friends, children and animals. *Sie* (sing. and pl.) is the polite form of address.

NOTE 1: *Du, ihr, dein, euer,* etc., are always written with capitals in letters.
NOTE 2: *Sie* is modern and should be replaced by *Ihr* (sing. and pl.) in older contexts and by *du* (sing.) or *ihr* (pl.) in biblical contexts.
NOTE 3: The reader, formerly addressed by the author as *du*, is now addressed as *Sie*.

(c) Remember that 'it' will be rendered by *er, sie* or *es*, etc., according to the gender of the noun 'it' refers to.

(d) The third person personal pronoun object is added after *wie* to render the English 'such as' in sentences like the following:

Sie trug Kleider, wie **sie** ihre Großmutter getragen hatte.
Er trug einen Hut, wie **ihn** sein Vater getragen hatte.

(e) The demonstrative pronoun *dessen* (m. and n. sing. gen.) and *deren* (f. sing. gen., and pl. gen.) usually replace *seiner* and *ihrer*, the genitive of *er, es* and *sie*, when things are referred to.

Er ist **ihrer** (*of her*) nicht würdig. Er schämt sich **dessen** (*of it*). Er sank auf **dessen** Armlehne (*the arm of it*).

(f) The genitive forms of *derselbe* are normally used to render the third person pronoun (referring to things or concepts) when preceded by a preposition governing the genitive, e.g. außerhalb derselben (= Familie).

(g) Note the following 'genitive' forms:

meinerseits, deinerseits, unserseits, etc. (*for my part, etc.*); meinetwegen (*for my sake; (certainly) for all I care, I don't mind*), deinetwegen
(*for your sake*), etc.; (um) meinetwillen (*for my sake*) (um) unsert-
willen, etc.; unsereins/unsereiner (*people like us*) darf es sagen.

(h) With some prepositions *da(r)-* is usually used instead of the accusative and/or dative of the personal pronoun when referring to things:

dafür (*for it, for them*), dahinter, darüber, darunter, (dicht) daneben
(*close to it*), obendrauf (*on the top of it*)

NOTE 1: Such compounds are not possible with the prepositions *außer, entlang,
gegenüber, ohne* and *seit*.

NOTE 2: In addition to their literal meanings some of these compounds have acquired
other quite distinctive meanings, e.g. **dabei** (*in doing so, at the same time, while*),
dafür (*in return*), **dagegen** (*on/to the contrary, on the other hand*), **nichts dagegen**
(*nothing in comparison*), **nichts dagegen haben** (*have no objection*), **darauf** (*there-
upon*), **obendrein** (*into the bargain*), **darum** (*therefore*), **dazu** (*in addition*).

NOTE 3: **Deswegen** (*on account of it, for that reason, that is why*), **demgegenüber**
(*compared to this*) **dessenungeachtet** (*despite that*):

(i) Note the following uses of *es*:

i   As the object or complement of the verb or standing for an adjective
already mentioned where English usually omits 'it' altogether.

Ich habe es nie versucht. Wie er es schon so oft getan hatte. Ich liebe
es, hasse es, ziehe (es) vor, dorthin zu gehen. Die Rolle des Willens ist
es, sich zu entscheiden (*the function of the will is to decide*). Sie ist so
schön, wie es ihre Mutter einmal war. In der Tanzstunde war er nicht
ein einziges Mal aufgeregt gewesen. Aber jetzt war er es (M. HAUS-
MANN).

ii Where *es* is the real subject which is retained even when it is not the
first word in the clause.

Es regnet. Gestern hat es geschneit.
Es geht mir gut. Mir geht es schlecht. Wie geht's Ihnen?
Es sind meine Freunde. Wahrscheinlich sind es meine Freunde.
Weißt du, daß es meine Freunde sind?
Es gibt einen Gott. Leute gibt es heute noch, die das behaupten. Hier
gibt es viel Obst. Weißt du, was es zum Essen gibt? Ihn gibt es nicht
mehr (*he no longer exists*).
Es gibt nichts mehr zu tun. Es gab einen Streit.

iii Where *es* is a purely anticipatory grammatical subject which is omitted
unless it comes first in the clause. Note that the number, singular or
plural, of the verb will depend not on *es* but on the real subject of the
clause.

Es ist kein Mensch da. Es sind keine Menschen da. Keine Menschen
sind da. Weißt du, daß kein Mensch da ist?

Es scheint die Sonne. Die Sonne scheint.

Es gehört Mut dazu, das zu behaupten, Das zu behaupten, dazu gehört Mut.

Es wurde lange getanzt. Bei uns wurde lange getanzt.

NOTE: **Es gibt** (*there is, there are*) followed by the accusative insists on the existence of a thing or person. **Es ist** (*there is*) and **es sind** (*there are*) followed by the nominative merely assert the presence of a thing or person. **Es gibt** also has the meaning of 'happens', 'occurs', 'comes about'.

iv The phrase: es war einmal (ein König) (*there was once upon a time* ...) always begins with the anticipatory *es*.

v With personal pronouns *es* never introduces the clause but follows the verb which agrees with the personal pronoun.

Du bist es (*it is you*). Sind Sie es? Er ist es, der das gesagt hat.

vi The common English construction: 'it is ... that ...' is not a normal construction in German and is omitted.
Thus:
'It is with regret that I must decline this offer' becomes in German simply: Mit Bedauern muß ich dieses Angebot abschlagen.

NOTE: *Es* as a direct object (unlike other pronouns) cannot be stressed by beginning the main clause with it. Where stress is required it is replaced by *das*. e.g. **Das** weiß ich nicht.

44 Possessive Adjectives and Pronouns

(a) For declension, see *89, 100*.

(b) Note that 'his' = *sein*, 'her' = *ihr* irrespective of the gender of the following noun. Thus: *seine Mutter, ihr Vater*.

(c) The expression 'of my, your, etc., own' can often be neatly rendered by *ein eigen(er)* ... Thus:

Ich habe einen eigenen Wagen/ein eigenes Rad.
Wir haben ein eigenes Haus (*a house of our own*).

(d) The possessive pronoun (of which there are three related forms: *meiner, der meine, der meinige*) agrees in gender and number with the noun to which it refers. In conversation *meiner*, etc., is more usual.

Deine Ausgabe ist teurer als meine/die meine/die meinige. Mit meinem (e.g. Wagen) fährt es sich schneller als mit deinem. Deiner (e.g. Hut) gefällt mir besser als ihrer. Dies ist mein Buch, das ist deines und das sind ihre (i.e. Bücher). Hier ist ihr Buch, wo ist seines.

(e) The genitive rarely occurs, being generally replaced by the construction *von*+dative:

Das ist eins von meinen (*one of mine*); ein Freund von mir (*a friend of mine*).

(f) Except when, as in (d) above, the subject is *es, das* or *dies* the possessive pronouns *mein, dein, sein, unser, euer* (but not *ihr* or *Ihr*) used predicatively are still occasionally, in elevated language, left uninflected.

Das Buch/der Hut/die Handtasche ist dein. Du bist mein.

(g) Die Sein(ig)en (*his people/family*), das Sein(ig)e (*his property*); du mußt das Dein(ig)e tun (*your share/bit*).

45 Reflexive Pronouns

(a) For declension, see 99.

(b) *Selbst* strengthens the reflexive pronoun and must be added after the third person genitive.

Er hat sich selbst verletzt. Er spottet seiner **selbst**.
Du traust dir selbst nicht. Jeder ist sich selbst der Nächste. Er lacht über sich selbst.

(c) The reflexive pronoun generally refers to the subject of the sentence. It can, however, sometimes correctly refer to the object of the sentence.

Er sah einen Turm vor sich (*in front of him*). Der Turm erhob sich vor ihm (*in front of him*). Er hörte sie zu ihm sprechen. *But:* Er hörte sie zu sich sprechen (*to herself*). Er überließ die beiden sich selbst (*to themselves*).

(d) Das ist ein Problem für sich (*a separate problem*). Er dachte bei sich (*to himself*). An sich (*essentially*) ist es ganz leicht. Das Ding an sich (*in itself*); an und für sich betrachtet (*regarded by itself*).

(e) The dative reflexive pronoun is also used to indicate the possessor when parts of the body and (sometimes) clothing are mentioned:

Ich wusch mir die Hände, putzte mir die Zähne. Sie zog sich die Jacke/die Schuhe/die Strümpfe an.

46 Reciprocal Pronouns

(a) Wir lieben uns/einander; wir sind uns/einander heute morgen schon begegnet (*one another*); sie lasen sich/einander vor (*to one another*).

(b) Sie denken aneinander; sie sprechen miteinander.

(c) Die Arme einer um des andern Schulter, durchschritten sie den Saal (*their arms round one another's shoulders*) (DIE ZEIT).

47 Interrogative Adjectives and Pronouns

(a) **Welcher** (declension, see 90)

Welchen (*which*) Roman hast du gelesen? Welches ist der höchste Berg. Welches sind die höchsten Berge? Welche Berge sind die höchsten?

(b) **Was für einer/was für welche; was für (ein)**

Was für einer (*what sort of one*) ist das? Was für welche sind das? Was für ein (*what sort of a*) Roman ist das? Was für Romane sind das? Was für Wein ist das? Mit was für einem Bleistift schreiben Sie?

(c) **Wer** (declension, see 96)

Wer ist das? Wer sind Sie? Wer sind diese Leute? Wer kommt? (*who is coming?*) Wer kommt alles? (*who are coming?*) Wen traf er? Wessen (*whose*) Handtasche ist das? Wem gehört diese Handtasche? An wen schreibst du?

(d) **Was** (declension, see 96)

Was ist er? Was sind diese Leute? Was sind das für Leute? Das sind Handwerker. Was meinst du? Wessen (*of what*) ist er schuldig? Woran (an was = *colloquial*) denkst du? Womit (mit was! = *colloquial*) schreibst du? Worin (*in what*) besteht der Unterschied? Worein (wohin *is more usual*) (*into what*) hast du es geworfen? Was (= warum, *colloquial use*) weint sie denn?

NOTE: *Welches/wer/was* with *sein* are complements, not subjects. Hence the person and number of the verb will depend not on them but on the following noun or pronoun. (Cf. 49(c) NOTE.)

48 Relative Pronouns, Adverbs and Clauses

(a) Relative clauses (with the finite verb coming last!) are introduced by the relative pronouns *der, welcher, so* (obsolete, poetical and indeclinable), *wer, was* (declension, see 95, 96) or by relative adverbs e.g. *wo, da, worüber, womit, um dessentwillen* (m. and n. sing.), *um derentwillen* (f. sing. and m. f. n. pl.), *dessentwegen*, etc., and, in elevated speech, *darin* etc.

(b) The relative pronoun, never omitted in German, agrees with its antecedent in gender and number.

(c) After the genitive of the relative pronoun (*dessen, deren*) the noun immediately following never has the definite article. (Cf. 'whose' in English.)

(d) The pronominal adverb forms *womit, worauf,* etc., are used with indefinite antecedents. They must never be used with an animate object antecedent, and with definite inanimate object antecedents the full form of the relative tends now to be preferred.

(e) The relative pronoun *welcher* is rarely used in spoken German. Its chief use is for the avoidance of ugly repetitions and as an 'elegant variation'.

(f) Examples of use:
i Der Mann, **der** gekommen **war**, hieß Hille.
   Das ist der Junge, **den** ich heute morgen **traf**.
   Das Mädchen, **dessen** Schwester krank **ist**, wohnt jetzt hier.
   Frau Meßner, bei **deren** Eltern wir **wohnen**, kam gestern.
   Die Kinder, mit **denen** wir gestern **spielten**, waren sehr nett.
   Das Messer, mit **dem** (*rather than:* womit) ich mich **schnitt**, . . .
   Eine Stille, **darin** das Leben . . . bemerkbar **ward** (G. HAUPTMANN).
   Mein Bruder, **um dessentwillen** (*for whose sake*) sie ihre Stelle aufgegeben **hat**, . . .
   Die Kleider, **derentwegen** (*because of which*) sie heute **vorbeikam**, . . .
   Der Grund, **weswegen/dessentwegen/warum/weshalb** er nicht gekommen **ist**, . . .
   Worte, **die** zu verstehen ich mir keine Mühe **gab**, . . . (*which I did not try to understand*).
   Pläne, von **denen** er **weiß**, daß er sie nicht wird ausführen können, . . . (*which he knows he will not be able to*).
ii Du, **der du** (*you who*) das **sagst**, lügst.
   Wir, **die wir** das nicht **glauben**, . . .
But Er, **der** (*he, e.g. Karl, who*) das **sagt**, . . .
   Ich bin es, **der** angerufen **hat** (*It is I who* . . .).
iii Das, was; dasjenige, was; dasselbe, was; das wenige, was; alles, was; vieles, was; manches, was; einiges, was; nichts, was; allerlei (mancherlei, vielerlei), was; etwas, was/das.
iv Das Beste, was (*the best thing*); das einzige, was (*the only thing*); das erste, was (*the first thing*).
v Das ist es/alles, woran ich mich erinnern kann.
   (Das,) worum es sich handelt, weiß ich nicht mehr.
   Nicht das, um was man kämpfte, . . .
   (Das,) worauf es ankam, habe ich jetzt vergessen.
vi Tue, was du kannst.
   Er erinnerte sich an das (*not:* daran), was ich gesagt hatte.
vii Er behauptet, was (= *a thing which*) ich nicht glaube, daß sie verheiratet ist.
viii Wer wagt, gewinnt. Wem nicht zu raten ist, dem ist auch nicht zu helfen. Wer sie aufmerksam las, kann nicht zweifeln, daß . . . (*Nobody who . . . can doubt*).
ix Dort, wo der Mann steht, . . . Überall, wo . . .
   Zur Zeit, da (*or* wo) . . .

49 Demonstrative Adjectives and Pronouns

(a) **Dieser, jener** (declension, see *90*).

Jener (in conversation usually replaced by *der da/dort*) is used chiefly in opposition to *dieser* and 'that' is otherwise rendered by, e.g. the demonstrative *der* or *dieser* followed later by *da/dort*.

Dieser Hut ist eleganter als jener/als der da. Mit diesem Auto fährt man schneller als mit jenem/als mit dem dort.

Helga und Irma sehen sich ähnlich, doch hat diese (*the latter*) blonde und jene (*the former*) schwarze Haare. (Cf. *31(d)iii*.)

Dies(es) und jenes (*this and that*); wir sprachen von diesem und jenem.

In jener schrecklichen Nacht, in der ... (*On that terrible night when ...*).

But Die/diese Schale dort (*that bowl*) möchte ich haben.

(b) **Solcher** (declension, see *90*); **so ein(er)** (sing. only); **derlei, derart, dergleichen** (all indecl.)

Solcher is declined strong (see *86(a)*), except when preceded by *ein*, when it is declined as in *92*. It is uninflected when followed by *ein*, and may remain uninflected when followed by an adjective.

Ich habe solchen (so einen) Durst, solche Kopfschmerzen.

Sie hatte solche Angst. Wir haben solches schlechte/solch schlechtes Wetter gehabt.

Mit solcher Anmut; mit solchem Ernst.

Ein solcher Mann, solch ein Mann, so ein (*such a*) Mann, solch junge Leute, solche jungen Leute.

Solche, die ... (*those who ....*).

So einer kann es nicht verstehen.

Derlei Überlegungen; derart Briefe; dergleichen Leute.

(c) **Der, die, das** (declension, see *97*); **dies** (indecl.)

Der (*he*) hat es getan. Die (*her*) kenne ich gut. Das ist deins, dies ist meins. Das (*those*) sind deine, dies (*these*) sind meine. Das/der/die bin ich. Ich bin dessen ganz sicher. Dem kann ich nicht widerstehen.

NOTE: *Der/die/das/dies* used with *sein* are complements, not subjects. Hence the person and number of the verb will depend not on them but on the subject. (Cf. *43(i)iii*.)

Der, der das behauptet ... (*he, the person, who*); die, die das behaupten, ... (*those (people) who*). Der (Mann) war es, der ... (*He it was (it was that man) who*). Viele **derer**, die ... (*many of those who*); unter denen, die ... (*among those who*); mit denen anderer Länder.

Dein Wagen fährt schneller als der deines Bruders (*your brother's*).

Mit deinem Wagen fährt es sich bequemer als mit dem deines Bruders.

Mein Bruder und dessen (*his*) Freund; ihre Schwester und deren (*her*, i.e. *the sister's*) Freundin.

Der einzige Grund dafür ist der, daß er nicht ausgehen will. Seine einzige Absicht ist die, kein Geld auszugeben.

(d) Derjenige (declension, see *94*)

Derjenige, der ... (*he, the person, the man, who*); diejenige, die ... (*she who*); diejenigen, die ... (*those, the people, who*); diejenigen Bücher, die ... (*those books that*); mit allen denjenigen, deren ... (*those whose*).

(e) Derselbe (declension, see *94*); der gleiche

Der gleiche means both 'identical' and 'similar', *dasselbe* only means 'identical'. When mere similarity needs to be shown *der gleiche* should be used.

Sie hatte denselben Hut auf wie gestern. Sie hatte den gleichen Hut auf wie ihre Schwester.

An demselben/am selben Tage *or* an dem gleichen Tage.

Es läuft/kommt auf dasselbe/das gleiche hinaus (*amounts to the same thing*).

(f) Selbst, selber (indeclinable)

Except in the phrase *von selbst* (of its own accord) *selbst* must be preceded by a noun or pronoun. *Selber* is more colloquial.

Ich selbst, wir selbst, Gott selbst.

Er ist nicht er selbst. Er denkt nur an sich selbst (selber).

Die Tür schließt sich von selbst.

50 Indefinite Pronouns

(a) Man

Like *on* in French, *man* (nominative only) is used where English has 'one', 'you', 'we', 'somebody', 'people', etc., or a passive construction. There is no genitive; the accusative is supplied by *einen*, the dative by *einem*.

Man ißt. Man kommt. Man sagt, daß ... (*it is said that*).

Hier verkauft man Zigaretten (*are sold*).

Was man/einer sagt, kann man nicht immer glauben.

Man hat seinen (*one's*) Stolz. Sie sollten einen in Ruhe lassen. Das steht einem ganz frei.

NOTE: *Man* is not interchangeable with *er, Sie, du*, etc. If you have started using *man*, go on using it consistently.

(b) **Einer; keiner** (declined strong, see *86(a)*, *100(a)*)

Eine(r) von euch muß gehen. Ich weiß eines (*one thing*). Der Titel eines (*of one*) der Bücher. In einem der Bücher. Ich habe es von einem/einer von euch. Keine(r) (*not one*) von euch darf ein Wort sagen. Gar keiner (*nobody at all*) wollte kommen. In keinem der Bücher. Sie ist meine Nina, keines sonst (*nobody else's*) (RINSER).

NOTE: *One(s)* is not translated when it occurs in English after an adjective: Die große Schale dort, die rote (*the red one*); die großen Schalen dort, die roten (*the red ones*). Dein Leben ist ein sehr volles (*a full one*).

(c) **Jemand; niemand**

Jemand (*somebody*) ist da. Kennst du jemand(en), der ... (*anybody who*). Das ist jemands Hut. Er spricht mit jemand(em). Ist sonst noch jemand (*anybody in addition*) gekommen? Jemand anders (*somebody else*, i.e. *different*) ist da. Er spricht mit jemand(em) anders. Niemand ist gebildet, der ... Niemand anders als (*other than*). Der Krieg ist niemands Schuld (HESSE).

(d) **Jeder, jedweder, jeglicher** (declined strong, *90*); **jedermann**

Jedweder is more emphatic than *jeder* and means 'every single' (*jeder einzelne*). It belongs to the literary language only. *Jeglicher* is becoming archaic and is used now only in elevated style. All except *jedermann* can be used adjectivally. *Jedermann* inflects only in the genitive.

Jeder/jedermann weiß das. Er nimmt jeden (*anybody*) an. Jedermanns Sache (*everybody's business*). Wir meinten jeder, daß ... (*we each of us thought* ...). Wie jeder andere (*like everybody/anybody else, any other*); jede beliebige Person (*any person whatever*). Jede(!) Ferien (*every holidays*).

(e) **Welcher** (declined strong, see *90*)

Er hat keinen Tabak. Hast du welchen (*any*)? Er hat keine Milch. Hast du welche? Er hat kein Geld. Gib ihm welches (*some*)! Er hat keine Zigaretten. Hast du welche?

51 Indefinite Numeral Adjective-Pronouns

a) **Alles** (*everything, all*) ist umsonst. Dies/das alles (*all this/that*) ist falsch. Dies/das alles (*all these/those*) sind triftige (*cogent*) Gründe. Ohne allen (*any*) Grund; trotz alles/allen Lärms; allen Ernstes (*in all seriousness*); mit aller Kraft. Trotz alledem (*despite all that*). **Alle** (*everybody, all*) sind gekommen. Sie sind alle gekommen. Alle anderen sind stehengeblieben. Alle diejenigen, die ... (*all (of) those who*).

All(e) diese Leute, all(e) meine Bücher.
Alle zwei Wochen (*every second week, every two weeks*).
Der Wein, die Milch, das Brot ist **alle** (*all gone, finished*).

(b) Ich will dir **etwas** (*or* **was**: *colloquial*) sagen. So etwas (*that sort of thing*) ist nur zu wahrscheinlich. So etwas Ähnliches (*something of that sort*); bei so etwas (*in that sort of matter*). Sonst etwas gefällig? (*is there anything else you would like?*) Er hat etwas anderes (*something else*) gekauft. Sprechen wir von etwas anderem.
Ich habe **nichts** gesagt.

(c) Gib mir **etwas** Brot, **ein bißchen** Brot, **ein wenig** Brot, **mehr** Brot, **weniger** Brot! Gib mir etwas, etwas mehr, ein bißchen mehr, ein bißchen weniger! Das ist **lauter** (*sheer*) Unsinn.

(d) **Viel(es)**, **nur wenig(es)**, **manches** (*quite a lot*), **einiges** war mir bekannt. Ich habe viel(es), zuviel, nur wenig(es), manches, einiges erlebt. Er hat viel (wenig) Humor, Zeit, Geld. Viel**en** Dank (= *only exception in the acc. masc.*). Er hat einigen Humor, einige Erfahrung. Er hat einiges Verständnis dafür. Mit wenig, viel Mühe, mit viel(er) Anstrengung, viel(em) Fleiß, mit wenig Eifer, mit einiger Anstrengung, mit einigem Fleiß; trotz der vielen Arbeit; wieviel Bücher?

(e) **Viele**, **zu viele**, **wenige**, **einige/etliche** (*some*), **mehrere** (*several*), **manche** (*quite a number*), **sämtliche**, **andere** junge Leute; die Stimmen vieler, weniger, einiger/etlicher, mehrerer, mancher, sämtlicher, anderer junger Leute; einige wenige Leute; wie viele Bücher?

(f) Sein **ganzes** Vermögen (*the whole of his fortune*); in dem **ganzen** Dorf; in **ganz** Berlin, Deutschland, Europa.

(g) **Die einen ... die anderen** (*some ... others*); mit den einen ... mit den anderen. **Nur die wenigen** wissen davon.

52 Prepositions governing the Accusative

(a) **ausgenommen** (*except*)
Alle rauchten, ihn ausgenommen.

NOTE: This word can also be used as a conjunction, e.g. alle rauchten, ausgenommen er; keinem hat er etwas angeboten, ausgenommen mir.

(b) **bis** (*till, by, to, as far as, right up to*)
Er bleibt bis nächsten Montag. Bis (*by*) nächsten Sonntag bin ich zurück. Bis morgen! (*see you tomorrow*). Zwei bis drei Stunden; von

Montag bis Mittwoch. Wir gingen bis zur Stelle, bis zum Ufer (*up to*). Bis zu diesem Tag, bis ans Ende der Welt, bis zum Ende des Reichs, bis (nach) Stuttgart. Alle kamen bis auf einen (*except one*).

(c) **durch** (*through, by*)

Er ging durch den Wald. Er wurde durch das Signal gewarnt.

(d) **entlang** (*along*)

Er ging die Straße entlang (*along, up, down the street*).

(e) **für** (*for, in relation to, for the benefit of, to the value of, by*)

Das ist genug für heute. Er ist kräftig für sein Alter. Er arbeitet für sie. Er kaufte für 2 Mark Äpfel (*worth of*). Schritt für Schritt; Tag für Tag (*by, after*). Er geht für (*colloquial*) vierzehn Tage nach Paris.

(f) **gegen** (*against, towards, approximately, about, compared to*); **wider** (*against;* literary, except in a few phrases).

Das war gegen (wider) meine Absicht, gegen (wider) meinen ausdrücklichen Befehl. Er tat es wider Willen (*reluctantly*). Er kam wider Erwarten (*against all expectation*). Wir fahren gegen Osten, Süden, Westen, Norden. Gegen 4 Uhr, gegen Ende des Monats, gegen 50 Verunglückte (*about*). Er ist nichts gegen Sie (*compared to you*).

(g) **ohne** (*without*)

Er tat es ohne mein Wissen.

(h) **um** (*round, exactly at, about, approximately at, by, for*)

Sie sitzen um den Tisch. Um 4 Uhr (*at*); um diese Zeit (*about*); um 1910 herum; Jahr um Jahr, ein Jahr ums andere (*by, after*). Er ist um einen Kopf größer als sie. Er ist um nichts gebessert. Um alles in der Welt nicht (*not for anything in*). Sie liefen um die Wette miteinander (*raced against one another*).

53 Prepositions governing the Genitive

(a)

abseits *off/away from*	diesseits *on this side of*
angesichts *in view of*	einschließlich *including*
anhand *with the aid of*	gelegentlich *on the occasion of*
anläßlich *on the occasion of*	halber *for the sake of*
(an)statt *instead of*	hinsichtlich *with regard to*
anstelle *in place of*	infolge *owing to, as a result of*
aufgrund *on the basis of*	inmitten *among, in the midst of*
ausschließlich *excluding*	innerhalb *inside, within*
außerhalb *outside*	jenseits *on the other side of*
bezüglich *with regard to*	kraft *by virtue of*

49

längsseits *alongside*
laut *according to*
(ver)mittels *by means of, with*
nördlich *to the north of*
ob *on account of*
oberhalb *above, higher up*
seitens *on the part of*
trotz[1] *in spite of*
um ... willen *because/for the sake of*
unbeschadet *without detriment to*
ungeachtet *in spite of*

ungerechnet *not including*
unterhalb *below, lower than*
unweit *not far from*
vermöge *by virtue/dint of*
von ... wegen *by the authority of*
während *during*
wegen *because of*
zeit *during*
zugunsten *on behalf of, in favour of*
zwecks *for the purpose of*

(b) *Examples:*

Außerhalb der Stadt, innerhalb der Stadt, oberhalb des Dorfs, unterhalb des Dorfs, der Brücke; innerhalb eines Monats.

Bezüglich derer, die ...; einschließlich der Kosten; der Ehre halber; inmitten der Häuser; kraft seines Amtes; laut seines Briefes; mitten während der Mahlzeit (*in the midst of*); zeit ihres Lebens; zugunsten der neuen Grundsätze. Nördlich/östlich/südlich/westlich des Flusses.

Um Gottes/Himmels willen; von Staats wegen; von Rechts wegen (*by right*).

Um meinetwillen/deinetwillen, etc.; meinetwegen, deinetwegen, etc. *or* (*colloquially*) wegen mir(!), *but not* wegen meiner.

Infolge des Krieges litten viele an Hunger.

But Wegen des Vaters habe ich nichts gesagt.

Er hat es statt meiner gemacht.

But Er hat es mir statt (*conjunction*) meinem Bruder gegeben.

Trotz des schlechten Wetters, *but:* trotzdem, trotz allem, trotz alledem.

54 Prepositions governing the Dative

(a) **aus** (*out of, from, of*)

Er ging aus dem Haus. Er ist aus der Schweiz. Er stammt aus guter Familie. Ich weiß es aus Erfahrung. Themen aus (*from*) Klopstocks Oden.

Es ist aus Leder, Glas, Eisen, etc. Aus (*for what*) welchem Grunde? Er tat es aus (*for*) Liebe, aus (*from*) Interesse, Vaterlandsliebe, aus Versehen (*by mistake, accident*), aus Gründen, die ... (*on grounds*), aus (*for*) Mangel, aus Furcht angetrieben (*actuated by fear*).

(b) **bei** (*at* (*the house of*), *near, with, among*(*st*), *in* (*the works of*), *by, on*)

Er wohnt bei seinem Vater. Die Schlacht bei (*of*) Leipzig; Potsdam bei Berlin.

[1] Also with dative

Er ist immer bei der (*at his*) Arbeit. Bei den Franzosen; bei Goethe. Bei (*by*) elektrischem Licht; bei (*in*) schlechtem Wetter.

Bei (*on*) meiner Ankunft, Rückkehr; bei näherer Prüfung (*on closer examination*); bei so etwas (*on this sort of matter*); bei der Veröffentlichung (*on publication*), bei dieser Gelegenheit (*on this occasion*); er hat keiń Geld bei (*on*) sich. Beim ersten Anblick (*at the first glance*); bei ihrem Anblick (*at the sight of her*); bei (*at*) jedem Schritt, jedem dritten Wort; bei (*at*) Tagesanbruch, Sonnenuntergang; beim Aussteigen (*on/ while getting out*); bei der Durchsicht (*on perusing, in his perusal*).

(c) **binnen** (*within*, of time)

Binnen einem Jahr, zwei Tagen, kurzem.

(d) **dank** (*thanks to*: also with the genitive)

Dank meinem Fleiße; dank dieser Maßnahmen (C. STERNHEIM).

(e) **entgegen** (*contrary to, against, towards*)

Er tat es entgegen meinen Wünschen/meinen Wünschen entgegen; entgegen allem Anschein (*contrary to (all) appearances*). Der Wind war ihnen entgegen. Dem Toten Meer entgegen.

(f) **entlang** (cf. 52(*d*)) (*along:* rarely follows noun)

Entlang dem Ufer, dem Ufer entlang waren ...

(g) **gegenüber** (*opposite; towards*, in figurative sense; *compared with*)

Er wohnt mir gegenüber, der Kirche gegenüber/gegenüber der Kirche. Mir gegenüber hat er sich immer anständig benommen. Er hatte mir gegenüber viel bessere Chancen gehabt.

(h) **gemäß** (*in accordance, conformity with*)

Deinem Wunsch gemäß, seinem Stande gemäß, den Gesetzen gemäß.

(i) **gleich** (*like:* also regarded as an adjective governing the dative, see 22(*d*))

Gleich mir hat er nichts gegessen.

(j) **längs** (*along:* also with the genitive)

Längs dem Wege (*or:* des Weges) stehen Bäume.

(k) **mit** (*with, in*)

Sie kam mit ihm. Sie winkte mit der Hand, mit dem Taschentuch (*waved*). Er fuhr mit der Hand (*passed his hand*) über die Stirn. Er fuhr mit der Hand (*put his hand*) in die Tasche. Er stieß ihn mit dem Fuß/dem Ellenbogen/der Faust (*kicked/nudged/punched*) Er schrieb

c

mit (*in*) Tinte, mit Bleistift. Mit Gewalt (*by force*), mit Absicht (*on purpose*), mit der Zeit (*in* (*the course of*) *time*), mit einmal (*all at once*), mit einem Schlag (*at one blow*), mit der Überzeugung (*under the conviction*); mit lauter Stimme (*in a*); mit anderen Worten.

(l) **nach** (*to* (*place*), *after, according to, to judge by*)

Er fuhr nach der Stadt, nach Bonn, nach Italien, nach Amerika, nach Hause (*home*).
Er kam nach (*after*) mir, nach einer Stunde; nach Christi Geburt (*A.D.*).
Nach meiner Ansicht, Meinung/meiner Ansicht, Meinung nach (*in my opinion*), nach Verdienst (*according to merit*), allem Anschein nach (*to all appearance*), der Reihe nach, (*in turn, in rotation*), seinen Jahren nach (*to judge by*); je nach dem Wetter/den Umständen (*depending on/according to, the weather/circumstances*). Ich kenne ihn dem Namen nach (*by name*). Er malt nach der Natur (*from nature*).

(m) **nächst, zunächst** (*next to*)

Es steht (zu-)nächst dem Bahnhof, dem Bahnhof zunächst; (*with pronouns*) nächst ihm, ihm zunächst.

(n) **nahe** (*near*: also regarded as an adjective governing the dative, see 22(*d*))

Sie stand nahe seinem Hause. Nahe der Erdoberfläche.

(o) **nebst, samt, mitsamt** (*together with*)

Die Mutter kam nebst/(mit-)samt ihren Kindern.

(p) **seit** (*since, for* (*length of time*))

Seit dem Krieg, seit seiner Abreise. Seit (*for*) einem Jahr wohnt sie bei uns.

(q) **von** (*from, of, by, out of*)

Er ist von Berlin nach Hannover gereist. Von Haus zu Haus, von Zeit zu Zeit. Die Königin von England. Ein Mann von 40 Jahren; ein Mann von Ehre; ein Mann von großer, kleiner Statur/Gestalt (*a tall, short man*).
Südlich, nördlich, westlich, östlich von (*to the south, etc., of*) Paris.
Ein Bild von (*by*) Dürer. Er wurde von ihm geschlagen.
Er ist von Geburt (*by birth*) ein Engländer. Ich kenne ihn von Ansehen (*by sight*), von Person (*personally*).
Eine Ausnahme von der Regel (*exception to*). Neun von zehn (*nine out of ten*).

(r) **zu** (*to, in, at*)

Er ging zu ihnen, zum Arzt (*doctor* or *doctor's*), zum Bahnhof, zur Post, zur Brücke, zum Dorf, zum Markt(-platz).
Er ging zu Bett. Bitte, zu Tisch! Er kam heute zu Hause an.
Er kam zu Fuß, zu Pferd, zu Rad, zu Schiff.
Er ißt bei uns zu Mittag, zu Abend.
10 Briefmarken zu (*at*) 20 Pfennig.
Zu unseren Lebzeiten (*in our lifetime*), zu (*in*) unserer Zeit, zu einer Zeit (*at one time, epoch*), zu Anbeginn (*at the very beginning*), zur rechten Zeit (*in time, punctually*), zu (*at*) Ostern, zu Weihnachten, zu Pfingsten.
Zu (*on*) beiden Seiten; zu meiner Rechten/Linken.
Zu unserem Schaden (*to our cost/loss*), zum Wohl (*for the good*) des Volkes, zum Unterschied von (*as distinct from, in contra-distinction to*), zur Not (*if need be*), zum Glück (*fortunately*), zum Beispiel, zur Frau geben/nehmen (*give/take in marriage*), zur Frau haben (*have as a wife*), zum Dichter geboren (*born to be*).
Das Wirtshaus zum Roten Adler (*The Red Eagle Inn*).

NOTE: 'To a person' (motion) is nearly always *zu*.

(s) **zufolge** (*in accordance with, according to*)

Ihrem Brief zufolge habe ich ...

(t) **zuwider** (*contrary to, against*)

Das ist dem Gesetz, Ihrem Versprechen zuwider.

NOTE: Er ist mir zuwider (= *adverb*) (*he is repugnant to me, I find him loathsome*)

55 Prepositions governing the Accusative or Dative

(a) *An, auf, außer, hinter, in, neben, über, unter, vor, zwischen* govern the accusative to indicate movement **to** a place, the dative to indicate rest or movement **at** a place, e.g.

Er setzte sich (*sat down*) auf **die** Bank; er saß (*was sitting*) auf **einer** Bank.
Das Flugzeug flog über (*flew across*) **die** Stadt; das Flugzeug kreiste über (*circled above*) **der** Stadt.

(b) When used idiomatically the same rule applies if the distinction can still be felt; otherwise the accusative is used after *auf, über*, the dative after *an, in, unter, vor, zwischen*.

The following are common idiomatic expressions:

(c) **an + accusative** (*on, to*)

Er ging ans Meer (*to the seaside*), an die Front; er setzte sich ans Feuer (*by the fire*). Sie kommen an die Reihe (*it is your turn*).

(d) **an** + **dative** (*at, on, by, along, in*)

Am nächsten Tag/Morgen/Abend ((*the*) *next* ...); an diesem Nachmittag (*that afternoon*); am Ende der Woche, am Wochenende.
Wir sind am Meer (*at the seaside*), nahe an (*near*) der Küste, am Kamin (*by the fireplace*); die Häuser am Ufer (*along the bank, on the shore*); an der Themse, der Mosel (*by/on the Thames, Mosel(le)*); an der Seite des Berges; am (*on, along*) Horizont; an dieser Stelle (*in, on, at this spot*); an deiner Stelle (*in your place, if I were you*); an meiner Seite (*at*); an meiner Linken, Rechten (*on*); was hast du an (*on*) der Schulter? Die Sterne am (*in*) Himmel; ein Professor an (*at*) der Universität.
Die Reihe/es ist an ihm (*it is his turn*); es ist an mir, es zu tun (*it is for me to* ...); es ist an der Zeit, daß ... (*it is time that*); alles, was sie an Seele besaß (*possessed in the way of soul*); das Schrecklichste an der Sache (*the most terrible thing about the matter*).

(e) **auf** + **accusative** (*on to, to, into*)

Er ging auf (*to*) die Post/Bank/Universität/den Markt, auf (*into*) die Straße.
Er ging auf die Jagd (*hunting*); er ging aufs Land (*into the country*); er zog aufs Land (*moved into*); er zog sich auf sein Gut zurück (*retired to his estate*).
Er ging auf (*for*) zehn Tage an die See; auf die Dauer (*in the long run*) ist das unmöglich.
Auf diese Weise (*in this way*), auf andere Weise, auf jeden Fall (*in any case*), auf Glück oder Unglück (*for better or worse*), er tat/versuchte es auf gut Glück (*he risked it*); er tat es auf eigene Kosten (*at his own cost*); auf den ersten Blick (*at first sight*).
Sage es auf (*in*) deutsch, englisch, französisch!

(f) **auf** + **dative** (*on, at, in*)

Er war auf (*at*) dem Markt, dem Bahnhof, auf (*in*) der Straße, auf dem Meer (*at sea, on/in the sea*), auf (*at*) der Post, der Bank. Er ist auf dem Lande (*in the country*).
Auf (*on*) seiner Reise, dem Rückweg, der anderen Seite.
Er wurde auf frischer Tat ertappt (*caught in the act*).

(g) **außer** + **accusative** (*beside, out of*)

Ich geriet außer mich vor Wut (*got beside myself*). Das setzt es außer allen Zweifel (*puts beyond all doubt*). Die Fabrik ist außer Betrieb gesetzt worden (*has been closed down*).

(h) **außer** + **dative** (*except for, out of, beside*)

Außer dir (*apart from, except for*) habe ich niemand.
Wir essen montags außer dem Haus (*eat out*). Er ist außer (*aller*)

Gefahr. Er ist außer Atem.

Ich war außer mir vor Freude, Wut, etc. (*beside myself with*).

(i) **hinter** + **accusative** (*behind*)

Er hat ihn hinters Licht geführt (*deceived, taken him in*).

(j) **hinter** + **dative** (*behind, beyond*)

Die Sonne verschwand hinter den Wolken. Er versteckte sich hinter einem Baum. Er kam hinter dem Schrank hervor (*came out from behind*). Das liegt hinter (*beyond*) Osnabrück.

(k) **in** + **accusative** (*into, to*)

Er kam in die Nähe (*near*), ging ins Freie (*into the open*), reiste ins Ausland (*went abroad*), fuhr in die Schweiz (*went to Switzerland*), flog in die Vereinigten Staaten (*flew to the United States*). Er ging ins (*to*) Theater, ins Kino, ins Konzert, in die Oper, ins Büro. Er brachte es wieder in Ordnung (*put it right*). Ich schnitt mich in den Finger (*cut my finger*).

(l) **in** + **dative** (*in, on*)

Er ist in der Nähe (*nearby*), im Freien (*in the open, out of doors*); er lebt im Ausland (*abroad*); in der Schule (*at school*); im Radio/ Fernsehen (*on*); im Grunde (genommen) (*basically*); ich bin im Bilde (*I see, I am in the picture*); ich ging im Haus ein und aus. In dem Augenblick (*at that moment*), im nächsten Augenblick (*the next moment*), im letzten Augenblick (*at*), in den Tagen der Verzweiflung, in einem anderen Jahr (*another year*), in (*on*) diesem Punkt, in einem Abstand/einer Entfernung von (*at an interval/distance of*), in regelmäßigen Abständen, in den Straßen Londons (*not* auf), im Gegensatz zu (*in contrast to, unlike*), im Durchschnitt, (*on the average*), im Dienst (*on duty*), im Schritt/Trott/Galopp (*at a walking pace, at a trot/gallop*), im leichten Galopp (*at a canter*), im wilden Galopp (*galloping madly*).

(m) **über** + **accusative** (*over, across*)

Er fuhr über (*via*) Ostende nach Köln. Er blieb über Nacht (*overnight*) bei uns. Das Jahr über (*throughout the year*); tagsüber; heute übers Jahr (*a year today*). Tränen liefen ihr über (*down*) die Wangen. Kinder über 8 Jahre; eine Rechnung über (*for*) 10 Mark.

(n) **über** + **dative** (*during; because of*, also with accusative)

Er schlief über dem Lesen ein; er vergaß den Dichter über dem/ den Menschen; er erwachte über dem Lärm.

(o) **unter** + dative (*among, between, under*)

Unter (*among*) den Leuten, meinen Papieren; unter anderem (*among other things*); unter uns gesagt (*between ourselves*).

Unter dieser Bedingung (*on this condition*), unter der Regierung (*in the reign*) Wilhelms II., unter diesen Umständen (*in/under these circumstances*), unter dem Vorwand (*pretext*), unter dem Namen K. bekannt (*known as K., by the name of K.*).

Unter (*during*) der Woche, der Predigt.

(p) **vor** + dative (*in front of, ago, outside*)

Vor (*ago*) vielen Jahren, vor langer Zeit, heute vor einem Jahr.
Vor allem/vor allen Dingen (*above all*).
Vor der Stadt (*just outside*); das liegt vor (*this side of*) Osnabrück.
Er lachte, weinte vor Freude (*for joy*). Sie zitterte vor Angst (*trembled with fear*), strahlte vor Freude (*beamed with, was radiant with*).
Er sieht den Wald vor (*for*) lauter Bäumen nicht.

(q) **zwischen** + dative (*between*)

Zwischen seinen eigenen vier Wänden (*within*).

56 Nouns and Adjectives with Prepositional Objects *(cf. 79)*

(a) Many nouns and adjectives take a prepositional object, i.e. either a noun or pronoun preceded by a preposition, or an adverbial compound;

der Glaube an Gott (*belief in God*); seine Abneigung gegen Arbeit, dagegen (*his dislike of work, of it*).

Er ist stolz auf ihn (*proud of him*); er ist zu allem bereit (*ready for anything*).

NOTE: The noun and adjective usually have the same prepositional constructions, but not invariably.

(b) See 79(*a*)*ii, iv* and 79(*v*) for clauses or gerunds as prepositional objects of nouns and adjectives.

The following list gives some of the most common examples where usage often differs from English:

(c) **an** + accusative (*to, of, in, on*)

die Anpassung (*adaptation*), der Anspruch (*claim/demand on s.b.*), die Bitte, der Brief, die Erinnerung, die Forderung (*demand on*), der Gedanke, der Glaube.

gewöhnt (*accustomed*).

(d) **an** + **dative** (*of, in, at, for, about*)

der Anteil (*share in*), die Anteilnahme (*regard, concern, sympathy for s.th.*), die Arbeit, der Bedarf (*need, requirements; stock*), die Freude (*joy, pleasure*), das Gefallen/Vergnügen (*pleasure*), das Höchstmaß (*maximum*), das Interesse, der Mangel (*lack*), das Mindestmaß (*minimum*), die Rache (*revenge*), die Teilnahme (*participation*), das Übermaß (*excess*), die Verheißung (*promise*), die Verzweiflung (*despair at*), der Vorrat (*supply of*), der Zweifel.

arm, ebenbürtig (*rivalling*), gewachsen (*a match for s.b. in*), (un)interessiert, jung, krank (*ill with*), reich, schuld (*to blame*), überlegen (*superior to s.b. in*).

(e) **auf** + **accusative** (*to, of, for, on, in*)

die Anspielung (*allusion to*), die Aussicht (*prospect of*), der Anspruch (*claim, pretension to*), die Antwort, die Anwendung (*application to*), der Blick (*view of*), die Eifersucht (*jealousy*), der Einfluß (*influence on*), die Hoffnung, die Jagd (*hunt, pursuit*), der Neid (*envy*), die Rücksicht (*consideration, thought for, of*), der Stolz, der Verlaß (*reliance*), das Vertrauen (*trust in*), der Verzicht (*renunciation*), die Vorbereitung, die Wirkung (*effect on*), die Zuversicht (*confidence*).

angewiesen (*dependent on, reduced to*), anwendbar (*applicable to*), aufmerksam (*attentive*), bedacht (*intent on*), böse (*angry with*), eifersüchtig, eingebildet (*conceited*), eitel (*vain*), erpicht (*keen*), gefaßt (*ready for*), neidisch, stolz, versessen (*mad about*), vorbereitet (*prepared for*), zornig (*angry with*).

(f) **auf** + **dative** (*in*)

blind, taub (*deaf*).

(g) **aus** + **dative** (*from, of*)

die Folgerung (*deduction*), die Mischung (*mixture*), die Übersetzung.

(h) **bei** + **dative** (*with, at, to*)

die Beliebtheit (*popularity*), der Besuch, die Hilfe,

anwesend (*present*), beliebt.

(i) **für** + **accusative** (*for, in favour of, of, in, to*)

das Beispiel, die Berechtigung (*excuse*), der Beweis, der Dank, die Entscheidung (*decision*), die Erklärung (*explanation of*), die Gefahr (*to*), der Grund, das Interesse, der Maßstab (*measure*), der Rat(-schlag) (*advice to*), die Sorge (*concern*), die Voreingenommenheit (*prejudice*), die Vorliebe (*predilection*), das Vorzeichen (*omen*), der Wunsch.

begabt (*good at*), bezeichnend (*characteristic*), empfänglich (*susceptible, receptive*), geeignet (*appropriate*), gefährlich, passend (*suitable*).

(j) **gegen** + **accusative** (*against, from, of, for, to*)

die Abneigung (*disinclination, distaste, dislike*), die Auflehnung (*revolt from*), die Einwendung (*objection*), die Entscheidung (*decision against*), die Feindseligkeit (*hostility*), das Gefeitsein (*immunity*), die Gleichgültigkeit (*insensitiveness, indifference*), die Grausamkeit (*cruelty*), die Güte (*kindness*), der Haß, das Heilmittel (*remedy*), die Klage (*complaint*), das Mißtrauen (*mistrust*), der Protest, die Unempfindlichkeit (*insensitiveness*), der Zorn.

allergisch, (un)empfindlich (*(in)sensitive*), feindselig, frech (*insolent*), gefeit (*proof against, immune to*), gefühllos (*insensitive*), gleichgültig, grausam, hart, (un)höflich, immun, mißtrauisch, nachsichtig (*indulgent*), streng, taub (*deaf to*), (vor)eingenommen (*prejudiced*).

(k) **gegenüber** + **dative** (*to, towards, with regard to*)

das Benehmen (*behaviour*), die Feindseligkeit (*hostility to*), das Geständnis (*confession*), die Haltung (*attitude*), die Pflicht (*duty*), die Unfreundlichkeit (*unpleasantness*), das Verhältnis (*relation*).

befangen (*ill at ease*), feindlich (*hostile*), schüchtern (*shy*).

(l) **in** + **accusative** (*in, into*)

der Einfall (*invasion of*), die Einmischung (*interference with*), die Einsicht (*insight*), Einweihung (*initiation*), die Ergebung (*resignation to*), der Rückfall (*relapse*), die Verwandlung (*transformation*).

eingehüllt (*wrapped*), eingeweiht (*initiated*), eingewickelt (*wrapped, of parcel*), gekleidet, vergraben (*buried*), verliebt (*in love with*), versunken (*sunk*), vertieft (*deep*), verwickelt (*involved in*).

(m) **in** + **dative** (*in, at, of*)

die Ankunft, die Bewandertheit (*knowledge*), die Kenntnisse (*pl.*).

beschlagen (*well up in*), bewandert (*versed*), geschickt (*skilled*), gewandt (*skilled*), gut, schwach, tüchtig (*efficient*).

(n) **mit** + **dative** (*with, in, for, to*)

die Ähnlichkeit (*likeness*), die Beschäftigung (*concern, occupation*), die Geduld (*patience*), die Freundschaft, das Mitleid (*sympathy, pity*), die Nachsicht (*allowance for, indulgence*), die Verbindung, der Vergleich (*comparison*).

bekannt (*acquainted*), einverstanden (*in agreement*), fertig (*finished, done*), (un)geduldig, streng, vergleichbar, verglichen (*compared to*), verlobt (*engaged to*), verheiratet, (un)verträglich (*(in)compatible*), vertraut (*familiar*), verwandt (*related*), zufrieden.

(o) **nach** + **dative** (*after, for, of, about*)

die Erkundigung (*enquiry*), die Frage, die Jagd (*pursuit* (*fig.*)), die Nachfrage (*demand*), die Sehnsucht (*longing*), das Streben (*aspiration*), die Suche (*search*), das Verlangen (*desire*), der Wunsch.

durstig, gierig (*avid*), habgierig (*covetous*), hungrig, sehnsüchtig.

(p) **über** + **accusative** (*about, as to, of, at, on*)

die Ansicht, die Bemerkung (*remark*), der Blick (*view over*), die Entrüstung (*indignation*), die Enttäuschung, die Freude (*joy*), der Gegenstand (*subject*), die Herrschaft (*mastery*), die Klage (*complaint*), die Meinung, die Neugierde (*curiosity*), der Rat(-schlag) (*advice as to*), die Rechnung (*bill for*), der Streit (*dispute, argument*), die Theorie, der Traum, der Überblick (*survey*), das Urteil (*verdict, judgment*), die Verhandlung (*negotiation*), der Vortrag (*lecture*), der Zweifel (*doubt*).

ärgerlich (*annoyed*), aufgebracht (*incensed*), bekümmert (*worried about s.th.*), bestürzt (*dismayed*), entrüstet, enttäuscht (*disappointed with, in*), erhaben (*above s.th., superior*), erstaunt, froh, neugierig, traurig, verlegen (*embarrassed at*).

(q) **um** + **accusative** (*for, on behalf of, about*)

die Bemühung (*exertion, effort*), die Bitte, der Kampf, die Sorge (*concern*), der Streit (*struggle, contest*).

bekümmert (*worried about s.b.*), besorgt (*worried, concerned*), verlegen (*at a loss for*).

(r) **unter** + **accusative** (*to*)

die Unterwerfung (*submission*).

(s) **von** + **dative** (*of, on, by, from*)

die Abhängigkeit (*dependence*), der Aufwand (*expenditure*), die Meinung, die Überzeugung (*conviction as to*), die Unabhängigkeit.

(un)abhängig, berührt (*affected*), entfernt (*far*), ergriffen (*moved, stirred*), frei, gerötet (*flushed*), müde, überzeugt (*convinced*), voll.

(t) **vor** + **dative** (*from, for, against, with*)

die Achtung (*respect*), die Angst, die Ehrfurcht (*reverence, veneration*), der Ekel (*loathing for*), die Furcht, die Hochachtung (*esteem*), der Respekt, der Schutz (*protection*), der Vorrang (*precedence over*), die Warnung.

blaß (*pale*), erschöpft, rot, sicher (*safe from*).

(u) **wegen** + **genitive** (*at, because of, by, for*)

bekannt (*known for*), berühmt (*famous for*), verlegen (*embarrassed by*).

(v) **zu** + **dative** (*to, for, of, (up)on*)

der Anlaß (*occasion*), der Beitrag (*contribution*), die Bereitwilligkeit (*readiness*), die Beziehung (*relation*), die Freundlichkeit, der Gegensatz (*contrast*), die Idee, die Liebe, die Lust (*desire, inclination*), der Mut, die Neigung (*tendency, inclination*), die Notwendigkeit, das Verhältnis (*relation*), die Vorbedingung, (*condition, prerequisite*), die Zeit, die Zuneigung (*affection, devotion*), der Zwang (*compulsion towards*).

ausgerüstet (*equipped*), berechtigt (*entitled*), bereit, entschlossen, freundlich, geeignet (*suitable*), geneigt (*inclined*), gut (*good to*), nötig.

57 Notes on *haben, sein, werden*

(a) Note the following irregular forms:

du hast, er hat; ich hatte, etc.

ich bin, du bist, er ist, wir sind, ihr seid, sie (Sie) sind; sei! seien Sie! seid!; ich sei, er sei; ich war, er war; ich bin gewesen.

du wirst, er wird; werde!; ich wurde, etc. (poetical forms: ich ward, du wardst, er ward); ich bin geworden.

(b) **Haben** is used to form the perfect tenses of all transitive and reflexive verbs and the modal auxiliaries. Exceptions are only apparent, being cognate or adverbial accusatives, old genitives, etc. (Cf. also (*d*) below.)

Er hat das Buch gelesen. Er hat sich gesetzt. Ich habe mir die Hände gewaschen. Er hat nicht kommen können.
But Er **ist** den Berg hinaufgegangen. Er **ist** die Wette eingegangen (*taken on the bet*). Er **ist** Gefahr gelaufen. Ich **bin** es losgeworden.

(c) **Sein** is used to form the perfect tenses of all intransitive verbs expressing the idea of movement to or from a place or of a change of state.

Er ist zum Bahnhof gegangen. Wir sind uns begegnet (*we met one another*). Er ist gestorben. Er ist krank geworden.

(d) **Haben** is used, with few exceptions, e.g. *sein, bleiben, geschehen, gelingen*, to form the perfect tenses of all intransitive verbs other than those excluded under (c) above.

Er hat geschlafen. Es hat geregnet.
But Es **ist** gewesen, geblieben, geschehen, gelungen.

(e) Some verbs can be used both transitively or intransitively or express different kinds of intransitivity. They are conjugated with *sein* if, when used intransitively, they fall under the rule given under (c) above.

Er **hat** den Wagen gefahren. *But:* Er **ist** mit dem Wagen gefahren.
Er **hat** viel getanzt. *But:* Das erste Paar **ist** ins Eßzimmer getanzt.

(f) There is a tendency to extend rule (c) above to include many intransitive verbs that express any form of movement, not just movement to or from a place.

Er **ist** den ganzen Tag geschwommen, geritten, gesegelt, gerudert, etc., *instead of:* er **hat** den ganzen Tag geschwommen, etc.

(g) Both *haben* and *sein* are occasionally omitted after the past participle in subordinate clauses.

... aus seiner Heimat, der er Ruhm geschenkt (s. zweig).

(h) **Werden** is used with the infinitive to form the future tenses, with the past participle to form the passive voice. (Cf. *69.*)

Er **wird/würde** das Lied **singen** (*will/would sing*).
Das Lied **wird/wurde** überall **gesungen** (*is/was sung*).

58 Notes on the Conjugation of Weak and Strong Verbs

(a) General:

i Strong verbs (see *102*) change their stem vowel, and the past participle ends in **-en**.

liegen: liegt, lag, gelegen.

ii Weak verbs do not change their stem vowel but add **-t** to the stem to form the imperfect, and the past participle ends in **-t**.

sagen: sagt, sagte, gesagt.

iii All verbs not stressed on the first syllable, i.e. the weak verbs ending in **-ieren** (a large number) and **-eien** (very few) and verbs compounded with inseparable prefixes (see *60(a)*) have no **ge-** in the past participle.

er hat studiert; sie hat prophezeit; wir haben versucht.

iv Verbs whose stem ends in **-t** or **-d** (except *(b)*v below), in **-chn**, **-ckn**, **-dn**, **-fn**, **-gn**, or **-tm** retain the **-e** of the 1st pers. sing. pres. indic. throughout the conjugation.

wartest, reitet, badet, rechnete, trocknete, ordnet, öffnetet, geregnet, atmet.

v A few verbs – *brennen, bringen, denken, kennen, nennen, rennen* and their compounds, and, but not always, *senden* and *wenden* with their compounds – are of mixed conjugation, i.e. though the stem vowel changes in the imperfect indicative and past participle to **a**, the imperfect has the weak imperfect endings and the past participle ends in **-t**.

brennen: brennt, brannte, gebrannt.
denken: denkt, dachte, gedacht.

vi There are very few irregular weak or strong verbs. The modal auxiliaries are given in *67* and the other irregular verbs in *102*. Note *wissen*:

pres. indic.: weiß, weißt, weiß, wissen, wißt, wissen;
impf. indic.: wußte, etc.; *past part.*: gewußt.

(b) The Present Tense:

i The present tense indicative endings of both strong and weak regular verbs are:

-e, -st, -t, -en, -t, -en.

ii With verbs whose stem ends in **-s, -ss, -ß, -z** or **-tz** the ending **-st** is either, and more usually, contracted to **-t** or is lengthened to **-est**.

du sitzt/sitzest; du liest/liesest.

iii Verbs ending in **-ern** and **-eln** (all weak) have the following present indicative endings:

-(e)re, -erst, -ert, -ern; -(e)le, -elst, -elt, -eln.

iv If the stem vowel of the infinitive of regular strong verbs is **a, e, o** or **au** it usually changes in the 2nd and 3rd pers. sing. pres. indic. to **ä, i/ie, ö** or **äu** respectively.

tragen: trägst, trägt; geben: gibst, gibt; lesen: liest; stoßen: stößt; laufen; läufst, läuft.

v Verbs so changing whose stem ends in **-d** or **-t** have the contracted endings **-st** and **-t** for the first type, **-st** and **-** for the second.

läd-st, läd-t; rät-st, rät.

(c) The Imperfect Tense:

i The imperfect indicative endings of strong regular verbs are:

-, -st, -, -en, -t, -en.

ii The imperfect indicative endings of weak regular verbs are:

-te, -test, -te, -ten, -tet, -ten.

(d) For the imperative forms see *65*; for the subjunctive forms see *70*.

59 Notes on the Tenses.

In general the tenses in German correspond to the English. There are however some important differences.

(a) **The Present**

i Since German has only one form of the present tense it is.sometimes necessary to add an adverb or to recast the sentence in order to convey the exact English meaning.

Jeden Tag geht er zur Stadt (*goes*). Sie pflegt spät aufzustehen (*gets up*). Er geht jetzt zur Stadt (*is going*). Er ist dabei, den Brief zu schreiben (*is writing*). Er ist beim Rasieren (*is shaving*). Es ist am Regnen (*it is raining*). Das Haus ist im Bau begriffen (*is being built*). Ich hoffe doch sehr, daß ... (*I do hope*). Selbst wenn wir arbeiten (*when we do work*). Er liebt mich tatsächlich/wirklich (*he does love me*).

ii With *seit* or *schon* the present expresses what has been going on and is still going on. Here English normally uses the perfect continuous. But the perfect is used (as in English) in negative sentences.

Er **arbeitet** seit heute morgen, seit acht Stunden (*has been working*). Ich **warte** schon eine Stunde (*have been waiting*). *But* Er hat seit Montag nicht gearbeitet.

iii The present is often used in German where English generally uses the future, especially when the idea of futurity is already indicated by some other means.

Morgen kaufe ich (*I shall buy*) welche. Ich schreibe (*I'll be writing*) dir bald.

iv The present tense is often used with a past meaning to give greater vividness. English normally prefers the past tense.

Noch immer stand er auf dem Gang. Er blickte zur Tür hinüber ... Er lugt durch den Spalt ins Zimmer ... Er horcht auf ... öffnet die Tür leicht und tritt mit seinen nackten Füßen völlig geräuschlos ins Zimmer (A. SCHNITZLER).

v Note also: Es ist höchste Zeit/an der Zeit, daß er **kommt** (*he came*); es ist das erstemal, daß ich Sie hier **sehe** (*I have seen you*).

(b) The Imperfect

i Jeden Tag ging er zur Stadt (*he went, used to go, would go*). Er pflegte früh zu Bett zu gehen (*would go, used to go*). Er las die Zeitung, als ... (*he was reading*). Er war schon dabei, den Brief zu schreiben (*was already writing*). Er war beim Rasieren (*was shaving*). Selbst wenn wir arbeiteten (*even when we did work*). Wir hofften doch sehr, daß ... (*we did hope*). In der Tat hatte er Erfolg (*he did succeed*). Er war im Begriff auszugehen, als ... (*he was on the point of*).

NOTE: The construction with *pflegte* should be used with discretion. It is not necessary to use it when an adverb or adverbial expression (e.g. *manchmal, oft, jeden Tag*) already indicates iteration. When there is a series of iterative verbs, once the German has made it clear, e.g. with the construction with *pflegte*, that the verbs are to be understood as having iterative meaning, the simple imperfect is normally adequate subsequently.

ii The imperfect is the normal tense of narrative.

Er stand auf, wusch sich schnell, kleidete sich hastig an und ging ohne zu frühstücken zum Bahnhof.

iii The imperfect with *seit* or *schon* expresses what had been going on and was still going on.

Er **arbeitete** schon seit acht Stunden (*had been working*).

Ich **wartete** schon eine Stunde (*had been waiting for*).

(c) **The Perfect**

i The perfect is used for isolated acts in the recent past where English often uses the simple past.

Ich habe heute angerufen (*I rang up*). Ich bin gestern gekommen (*I came*). Er ist eben nach Hause gekommen (*has just come*).

ii The perfect is used to express an event whose effect is still felt today.

Die Bundesrepublik ist 1954 ein souveräner Staat geworden (*became*).

iii In colloquial German, especially in South Germany, the perfect is the tense of narrative.

iv The perfect expresses a future perfect when the idea of futurity is already indicated by some other means. (Cf. (*a*)*iii* above.)

Ich habe das Buch bald zu Ende gelesen (*shall soon have finished*).

(d) **The Pluperfect**

The German pluperfect is used as in English except as shown in (*b*)*iii* above. Sometimes however it will render the English imperfect, e.g.

Früher war er Buchmacher gewesen (*he used to be*).

(e) **The Future**

i Der Arzt wird kommen müssen (*will have to*).
ii Aber müde wirst du sein (HESSE). (*But I expect you are tired*).
iii Note the following equivalents to the future and compare also (*a*)*iii* above:

Die Sonne will eben untergehen (*is just about to*).
Er ist im Begriff, nach Paris abzureisen (*on the point of*).

iv Note that when 'will' expresses determination or desire the present of *wollen* is used.

Er **will** nicht kommen (*he won't* = *refuses to*). **Willst** du auch kommen?

(f) **The Future Perfect**

Er wird das wohl gesagt haben (*I expect he said that*).

(g) **The Conditional; the Future in the Past**

i Er würde kommen, wenn er könnte (*would come* = *conditional*).
ii Ich wußte, daß er kommen würde (*would come* = *future in the past*).
(N.B. For (i) and not for (ii) *käme* may be substituted.)

64

iii Note that when 'would' expresses determination the imperfect of *wollen* is used; when it indicates habitual action, the imperfect of the main verb alone is used.

Er **wollte** nicht kommen (*he would not come = refused to come*).

Er **kam** jeden Abend um sechs nach Hause (*he would come = used to come*).

(h) **The Conditional Perfect**

This cumbrous form is usually replaced by the pluperfect subjunctive. Thus:

Ich hätte es gemacht *instead of*: ich würde es gemacht haben.
Er hätte es tun können *instead of*: er würde es haben tun können.

60 Compound Verbs

(a) All compound verbs are separable except (i) those compounded with the inseparable prefixes **be-, emp-, ent-, er-, ge-, miß-, ver-** and **zer-**, and (ii), with certain meanings only, those compounded with **durch-, hinter-, über-, um-, unter-, voll-, wider-** and **wieder-** (only in the one word *wiederholen* = repeat).

(b) The inseparable prefixes are never stressed, there is no *ge-* in the past participle and the *zu* of the infinitive construction is not inserted between the prefix and the verb.

er hat bezáhlt; er hat gewónnen (*from* gewinnen);
er hat übertríeben; es ist zu bezáhlen.

(c) The prefix *miß-* is sometimes treated as a separable prefix in the past participle and in the infinitive with *zu*.

míßgeachtet/mißáchtet; míßzuachten/zu mißáchten.

(d) Common examples of inseparable verbs belonging to (*a*)*ii* above are:

durchzíehen (*traverse a country*)
hintergéhen *deceive*
hinterlássen *bequeath*
überfáhren *run over s.b.*
überhólen *outstrip; overhaul*
überréden *persuade*
überráschen *surprise*
übersétzen *translate*
übertréiben *exaggerate*
überwínden *overcome*
überzéugen *convince*
umármen *embrace*
umfássen *comprise*
umgében *surround*

umgéhen *evade*
unterbréchen *interrupt*
unterhálten *entertain, maintain*
unternéhmen *undertake*
unterríchten *instruct, teach*
unterschéiden *distinguish*
untersuchen *investigate*
vollénden *complete*
vollführen *carry out*
widerlégen *refute*
widerspréchen (D) *contradict*
widerstéhen (D) *resist*
wiederhólen *repeat*

(e) Meaning and function of the inseparable prefixes ((a)i)

i **be-** makes intransitive verbs transitive and transitive verbs perfective in meaning: steigen – besteigen; decken – bedecken (*cover all over*);

from nouns forms verbs with the meaning 'provide with', 'endow with', 'give': Freund – befreunden; Glück – beglücken; Glückwunsch – beglückwünschen (*congratulate*);

from adjectives forms verbs with factitive meaning: lustig – belustigen (*make s.b. merry*).

ii **ent-** from nouns, adjectives or other verbs forms verbs expressing the idea of deprivation, separation, escape (cf. English 'de-', 'dis-', 'des-', 'un-', and 'away'): Kleid – entkleiden; mutig – entmutigen; decken – entdecken; kommen – entkommen;

from other verbs forms verbs with inchoative meanings: springen – entspringen ((*a)rise*).

iii **er-** from other verbs forms verbs with inchoative meaning or expressing successful completion or conclusion (sometimes with death as a consequence!): wachen – erwachen (*awake*); werben (*sue for, woo*) – erwerben (*acquire*); schießen – erschießen (*shoot dead*);

from adjectives forms verbs with inchoative or factitive meaning: blaß – erblassen (*turn pale*); frisch – erfrischen (*refresh*).

iv **ge-** from other verbs forms verbs with perfective or intensified meaning: brauchen (*need*) – gebrauchen (*use*); reuen – gereuen. (N.B. *ge-* is no longer a productive prefix.)

v **miß-** corresponds to English 'mis-', 'dis-': verstehen – mißverstehen; trauen – mißtrauen.

vi **ver-** from other verbs forms verbs with perfective or intensified meaning: treiben – vertreiben (*drive away s.b.*); schließen – verschließen (*lock up*); zweifeln (*doubt*) – verzweifeln (*despair*); sprechen – versprechen (*promise*);

from other verbs forms verbs expressing the idea of progress to completion or destruction: arbeiten – verarbeiten (*elaborate*); hungern – verhungern (*starve to death*); hallen (*echo*) – verhallen (*die away*);

from other verbs to form verbs with opposite meaning: achten (*esteem*) – verachten (*despise*); kaufen – verkaufen; mieten – vermieten;

from other verbs forms verbs expressing various ways time is spent: bringen – verbringen; schlafen – verschlafen; trinken – vertrinken;

from other verbs forms reflexive verbs implying one has bungled something: laufen – sich verlaufen (*lose one's way*); rechnen –

sich verrechnen (*miscalculate*); sprechen – sich versprechen (*make a slip of the tongue*);

forms transitive from intransitive verbs: folgen – verfolgen (*pursue*); lachen – verlachen;

from adjectives (including comparatives) forms verbs with inchoative or factitive meaning: alt – veralten; dünn – verdünnen (*thin down*); größer – vergrößern;

from nouns forms verbs with the meaning of 'provide with' or 'turn into': Silber – versilbern (*silver plate*); Film – verfilmen.

vii **zer-** expresses the English 'into pieces' and forms verbs chiefly from other verbs and from a few nouns and adjectives: reißen – zerreißen; Trümmer – zertrümmern (*reduce to ruins*); klein – zerkleinern;

from other verbs forms verbs with intensified meaning: knittern – zerknittern (*crease all over*).

(f) All prefixes other than those given in (a) above are separable and stressed.

(g) Most separable prefixes are simple or compound adverbs: *ab-, hinab-*. Some are adjectives as in the verbs *festbinden, freimachen, geringschätzen, hochachten, loslassen, totschlagen, vollaufen, wahrnehmen* (perceive), *weiterfragen*. The remainder are nouns as in the verbs *achtgeben, danksagen, fehlschießen, haltmachen, heimfahren, hohnlachen, maschineschreiben* (type), *preisgeben* (expose), *radfahren, skilaufen, standhalten, stattfinden, teilnehmen*.

(h) Note the most frequent meanings of some of the adverbial prefixes (see also *35(d)*):

ab (*off, away/down*)	Er schnitt es ab. Der Berg fiel steil ab.
an (*on, at*)	Er zieht es an. Er schaltet es an (*switches on*). Er sah ihn an.
auf (*up, open*)	Er steht auf. Er sah zu ihm auf. Er macht die Tür auf.
aus (*out, off, up*)	Er geht aus. Er zieht es aus. Er füllte das Formular aus (*filled up*).
ein (*in*)	Er steigt ein. Er trat ein.
empor (*up(-wards)*)	Er blickte empor. Er strebt empor. Er hob die Hände empor.
fort (*away, on*)	Er geht fort. Er lebt fort.
entgegen (*to meet*)	Er ging ihr entgegen.
nieder (*down*)	Er fiel nieder.
vor (*forward*)	Er trat vor.
voran/voraus (*on ahead*)	Er geht voran/voraus.
vorbei/vorüber (*past*)	Er geht vorbei/vorüber.
zu (*to, shut*)	Er rief mir zu. Er machte die Tür zu.

67

(i) For word order with separable compound verbs see 6(*g*).

(j) Compound verbs with double prefixes, the second being inseparable, have no *ge-* in the past participle, e.g.

> Er erkennt an (*acknowledges*); er hat anerkannt; er wünscht anzuerkennen.

Likewise: anvertrauen (*entrust*); auferlegen (*impose*); vorbehalten (*make reservations*); vorenthalten (*withhold*).

(k) Other compound verbs with double prefixes are treated as inseparable, e.g.

> Er überanstrengt sich (*over exerts himself*); er hat sich überanstrengt; ohne sich zu überanstrengen.

61 Reflexive Verbs

(a) The reflexive pronoun (see *45* and *99*) is rarely used except in the accusative or dative. Only the first and second person singular show the difference.

> Ich wasche **mich**. Ich wasche **mir** die Hände.
> Stell **dich** vor (*introduce yourself*)! Stell **dir** mal vor (*just imagine*)!
> *But* Stellt **euch** (D) mal vor! Erkältet **euch** (A) nicht!

(b) The German reflexive verb has often to be used where English uses an intransitive verb.

> Die Tür öffnete sich (*opened*). Sie trafen sich (*met*). Die Tür schließt sich von selbst (*shuts*). Er drehte sich um (*turned round*). Er wusch sich (*washed*). Er setzte sich (*sat down*). Er zog sich an (*dressed*). Er zog sich aus (*undressed*). Er zog sich um (*changed*). Sie irren sich (*you are wrong*). Er fühlte sich beleidigt (*felt insulted*).

(c) The English passive is sometimes rendered by a German reflexive verb (see *69(h)i*)

> Solche Bilder verkaufen sich schnell (*are sold*).

(d) Note the common German idiom in which the reflexive verb is used in impersonal constructions like the following:

> Es fährt sich bequem in diesem Wagen (*it is pleasant driving in*).
> Es schreibt sich schlecht mit Kreide (*chalk is difficult to write with*).

62 Impersonal Verbs

(a) Es blitzt, dämmert, donnert, dunkelt, friert, hagelt, regnet, schneit, klärt sich auf (*is clearing up*), taut (*is thawing; dew is falling*).

(b) So gut es geht (*as well as one can*); es geht (nicht) (*it will (won't) do*); es gibt; es heißt, daß (*it is said that*); es klingelt; es klopft; es handelt sich um (*it is a matter of*); es kommt darauf an (*it depends; that is what matters*); es lohnt (sich) kaum (*it is hardly worth while*); es macht/schadet nichts (*it does not matter*); es zieht (*there is a draught*).

(c) Mir fehlt es an nichts (*I lack nothing*); mir gefällt es dort (*I like being there*); mir geht es gut, schlecht, ausgezeichnet, etc.; mir gelingt es, das zu tun (*I succeed in, manage to*); dir geschieht es recht (*it serves you right*); dir steht es frei, das zu tun (*you are free to*); mir tut es leid (*I am sorry*). *Or:* Es fehlt mir an nichts, *etc.*

(d) Mir ekelt('s) vor ihm (*I loathe him*); mir/mich schaudert('s) vor dir, mir graut('s) vor dir (*I shudder to look at you*); mich/mir juckt('s) am Arm, am Finger, im Ohr (*my arm, etc., itches*); mich friert('s) an den Füßen; mich fröstelt('s). *Or:* Es ekelt mir vor ihm, *etc.*

(e) Mich dürstet nach (*I thirst for*); mir fällt ein, daß (*it occurs to me that*); mir ist, als ob (*I feel as if*); mir fehlt nichts (*I am quite well, I want, need, am short of nothing*); mich hungert; mir ist kalt, warm, übel, schlecht; mir ist bange, wohl, etc. zumute (*I feel apprehensive, in good spirits*); mir ist übel (*I feel sick*); mich verlangt nach (*I feel drawn towards*); mich wundert (*I am astonished*). *But:* Es dürstet mich nach, es fällt mir ein, daß, *etc.*

63 The Infinitive with and without *zu*

(a) The simple infinitive stands

i   after the modal auxiliaries:

Er kann es tun (*is able to*). Er mußte sich setzen (*had to*). Er wollte schreiben (*wanted to*). Er möchte kommen (*would like to*).

ii   after *bleiben, fühlen, gehen, heißen* (bid), *hören, lassen* (cf. *68*), *machen* and *sehen*:

Er blieb dort stehen. Er fühlte sich erröten. Sie ging tanzen. Er hieß ihn kommen. Ich hörte/sah ihn kommen. Er läßt alles herumliegen. Er machte sie erröten.

iii   after *lernen, lehren* and *helfen* when these follow their dependent infinitive; and in simple short sentences even when these precede.

Sie hat kochen gelernt, mich kochen gelehrt. Um den Krieg gewinnen zu helfen, hat er ...
Sie half uns aufräumen.

iv after *haben* in such expressions as:

Man sollte keine Spiegel herumhängen haben, keine Stühle herumstehen haben, keine Papiere herumliegen haben (*have hanging, standing, lying around*).
Du hast gut lachen/reden (*it's all very well for you to laugh/talk*).

v when used as a predicative accusative:

Das nenne ich Eulen nach Athen tragen (= *carrying coals to Newcastle*).

vi in abbreviated questions, direct or indirect, with modal verb usually understood:

Was jetzt anfangen? Er wußte nicht, wohin gehen.

(b) The infinitive with *zu* is used

i after *lernen, lehren* and *helfen* when these precede their dependent infinitive:

Er hat endlich gelernt, sich gut zu benehmen.

ii after all verbs and verbal expressions not excluded under (a) above:

Er wünschte, länger zu bleiben. Er vermochte nicht, sie zu überzeugen (*was unable to*). Es ist ganz unnütz, darüber zu streiten (*quite useless to*). Ich habe viel zu tun. Er scheint unglücklich zu sein.

iii after *ohne, (an)statt* and *weit (davon) entfernt*:

Ohne aufzublicken; statt zuzuhören; weit davon entfernt, ihn zu hassen, liebt sie ihn (*far from hating*).

(c) Usage fluctuates in the following cases:

i With the infinitive used as the subject of a sentence:

Ihn allein lassen, das wäre das Klügste (SCHNITZLER).
Euch zu helfen ist mein größter Wunsch (DUDEN).

ii after *nichts (weiter, mehr) als*:

Wir konnten nichts tun als auseinandergehen (HESSE).
So habe man ihr denn nichts mehr antun können, als eben ihr Bild aus dem Rahmen zu nehmen (LE FORT).

iii after *brauchen*:

Du brauchst nicht (zu) schreiben.

(d) *um ... zu* with the infinitive is used:

i to express purpose (*in order to, so as to*), though *um* is often omitted with *kommen*:

Er tat es nur, um mich zu ärgern. Er kam zum Bahnhof, (um) mich abzuholen.

ii after *zu* + adjective and usually after *genug* (+ adjective), *genügen, ausreichen, brauchen, bedürfen*:

Er war zu gut erzogen, um sie zu unterbrechen (LE FORT).
Ich war nicht schnell genug, um die Chance zu ergreifen (ANDERSCH).

iii to render 'enough to make' (cf. *80(c)*):

Es war um sich die Haare auszuraufen, um aus der Haut zu fahren
(*jump out of one's skin*), um verrückt zu werden.

(e) For the translation of such phrases as 'there was nobody, etc., to ...',
'it was too wet for us to ...' see *73(b)ii*.

64 The Participles

(a) Present and past participles are used attributively in German as extensively as in English.

Er bekam einen tröstenden Brief. Gebranntes Kind scheut das Feuer.

(b) Present and past participles are used predicatively in German much as
in English though a good deal less extensively. Normally the participle
comes at the end of its construction.

i Der Junge, vor Freude strahlend, bedankte sich.
Suchend blickte ich mich um (GRASS).
Die Arme verschränkend, stellte sie sich vor mir auf (BROCH).
... stampfte ich taktgebend die vier Treppen hoch (GRASS).
Meine Mutter, die Hölle fürchtend, wollte dort nicht einziehen
(GRASS).
Bier, Blutwurst mit Zwiebel bestellend, breiteten wir die Aufnahmen
aus (GRASS).
ii Da ruhte, eingeschmiegt in das Weiß, das schneedachige Oberdorf
(BROCH).
Den beiden anderen zugewendet, wiederholte er ... (BROCH).
Obgleich innerlich entrüstet, erklärte er es ihm ruhig.
So betrachtet, sieht die Sachlage anders aus.
Unten auf der Landstraße angekommen, machte Joseph halt (R.
WALSER).

(c) Present and past participles can be used in adjectival adjunct constructions where English uses either a following participle, a relative clause or
adjectival construction. This construction is sometimes very convenient,
but it should be used with discretion.

Wir sind jetzt in einer 200000 Bände umfassenden Bibliothek (*library
containing*).
Er betrachtete die neben ihren Pferden abgesessenen Reiter (*troopers
who had dismounted*) (SCHAPER).

71

(d) The present participle of transitive verbs when preceded by *zu* and declined has modal and passive force. This construction should also be used with discretion.

Die immer wieder an allen Schweizer Straßen **zu finden**·**le** Mahnung (*that is to be found*) ...
Er bereitete sich auf das nun nicht mehr **zu umgehende** Geständnis vor (*that could no longer be evaded*) (HEIMERAN).

(e) After *kommen* the German past participle corresponds to the English present participle after 'come'.

Er kam gelaufen (*running*), galoppiert (*galloping*).

(f) The past participle, but not normally a present participle, may introduce a noun clause in German, i.e. 'disappointed that ...' but not: 'remembering that'. Note however that *gesetzt* (*daß*) and *angenommen* (*daß*) translate the English present participle 'supposing'.

Enttäuscht, daß sie nicht gekommen war, ging er wieder nach Hause.
Gesetzt, er käme heute. Angenommen, daß es sich so verhält.

(g) See *32(a)* for the adverbial use of the participles.

(h) See *81* for further ways of translating the English present participle.

65 The Imperative

(a) Sag(e)! sagt! sagen Sie!; komm(e)!, kommt! kommen Sie!

(b) Du schläfst – schlaf(e)!; du stößt – stoß(e)!; du läufst – lauf(e)! *etc.*
But du gibst – gib!; du liest – lies! *etc.*

(c) Zitt(e)re nicht! hand(e)le! reinige!

(d) Geh du/geht ihr voran! (Cf. English imperative: *you* go on ahead.)

(e) 'Let us go' = gehen wir! wir wollen gehen! laß, laßt, lassen Sie uns gehen!

(f) Aufstehen! (*get up*). Ausgehalten! (*stick it out*). Wirst du still sein! (*be quiet*).

(g) Note the effect on imperatives of such words as *doch* (urging), *ja* (reminding), *mal* (emphasising), *nur* (persuasive, reassuring, sometimes threatening):

Kauf sie doch! (*Go ahead and buy.*) Hör doch! (*Do listen.*) Iß ja nicht zu viel! (*Mind you don't eat too much.*) Hör mal (zu)! (*Now just listen.*) Komm nur! (*Come on.*)

(h) Note that the imperative is generally followed by an exclamation mark.

66 The Interrogative

(a) Kennst du ihn? Wo hast du ihn kennengelernt?

(b) Du kennst ihn, nicht wahr (*don't you?*)? Du bist krank, nicht wahr (*aren't you?*)? Du hast schon gehört, nicht wahr (*haven't you?*)? Du wirst kommen, nicht wahr (*won't you?*)?

(c) Du kennst ihn schon, ja/nicht/gelt? (= *colloquial forms*).

(d) Du hast doch nicht gewartet? Doch (*yes I did*)!

67 The Auxiliary Verbs of Mood

(a) Er hat es gedurft, gekonnt, gemocht, gemußt, gesollt, gewollt
But Er hat kommen **dürfen, können, mögen, müssen, sollen, wollen.**

(b) **dürfen** (darf, darfst, darf, dürfen, etc.; durfte, etc.)
   Er darf jetzt wieder rauchen (*may, is allowed to*).
   Er darf nicht rauchen (*must not, is not allowed to, may not*).
   Darf ich rauchen? – Du darfst.
   Sie dürfen es nur sagen (*you need only say so*).
   Er durfte alles machen (*he was allowed to do anything*).
   Er durfte jahrelang nicht schwimmen (*was not allowed to swim*).
   Das dürfte alles sein (*that, I think, is everything*).
   Welcher Mensch dürfte den Zeitpunkt bestimmen (*should be allowed to*)?
   Es dürfte ein Leichtes sein (*should be an easy matter*).
   Es dürfte zwischen ihnen kaum Differenzen gegeben haben (*there can hardly have been*).
   Es dürfte wohl wahr sein (*it may well be true*).
   Er hat nicht kommen dürfen (*has not been, was not allowed to come*).
   Er hätte kommen dürfen (*would have been allowed, entitled to come*).
   Er hätte das Haus nicht verlassen dürfen (*should not have left, should not have disobeyed orders and left*).
   Er wird wohl kommen dürfen (*he will be allowed to come all right*).

73

(c) **können** (kann, kannst, kann, können, etc.; konnte, etc.)

Ich kann schon lesen (*can, am able to*).
Kannst du es beweisen? Ja, ich kann (es) (*I can*).
Du kannst bleiben (*can, may*).
Es kann sein (*it may be*).
Er kann (kein) Deutsch, Französisch, Italienisch, Russisch (*knows*).
Ich kann nicht mehr (*I can't go on any more, I'm finished*).
Ich kann nichts dafür (*I cannot help it*).
Ich kann nicht umhin zu lachen (*cannot help laughing*).
Du kannst das unmöglich sagen (*you cannot possibly*).
Er kann es getan haben (*he may have done it*).

Ich konnte nicht kommen (*could not, was unable to*).
Ich konnte nicht anders als lachen (*could not help*).
Ich konnte es ja getan haben (*I might have done it, it was possible after all that I did it*).

Er könnte wohl finden, daß ... (*might find that ...*).
Ich könnte es dort (vielleicht) kaufen (*could, might be able to*).
Du könntest es schon mitnehmen (*you might as well take it*).
Er könnte es getan haben (*he might have done it for all one knows*).

Er hat nicht kommen können (*has not been able, could not*).

Du hättest ebensogut kommen können (*you might as well have come*).
Er hätte kommen können, wenn ... (*could/might have come if ...*)
Du hättest es mir doch sagen können (*you might have told me = a reproach*).

Sie werden nicht kommen können (*they will not be able to come*).

(d) **mögen** (mag, magst, mag, mögen, etc.; mochte, etc.)

Er mag es vielleicht wissen (*he may perhaps know it*).
Er mag kommen (*may*). Das mag wohl sein (*may*).
Man mag sie vielleicht nicht leiden (*one may not like them*).
Was er auch tun mag (*no matter what he does*).
Mag man sie als Atome oder anders bezeichnen (*whether ... or*).
Er mag 2 Jahre alt gewesen sein (*may have been*).
Er mag gern kommen (*likes coming*).
Er mag nicht abreisen (*does not like*).
Ich mag sie nicht (*I don't care about them*).

Möge er lange gedeihen (*long may he flourish*)!

Was mochte er von mir halten (*what might he think of me*)?
Welche Talente er auch haben mochte (*might have had*).
Es mochte schon 11 Uhr sein (*may have been*).
Er mochte es wohl bemerkt haben (*might well have noticed*).
Er mochte gern zu uns kommen (*liked coming*).

Das ist mehr, als man zuerst annehmen möchte (*might suppose*).
Ich möchte länger bleiben (*should like to*).
Ich habe ihn später auch nicht gemocht (*did not like*).
Sie hätte schreien mögen (*would like to have screamed*).
Das hätte ich nicht sehen mögen (*should not have liked to*).
Er hätte glauben mögen, daß ... (*would have felt inclined to*).

(e) **müssen** (muß, mußt, muß, müssen etc.; mußte, etc.)

Er muß gehorchen (*must, has to*).
Kinder müssen gehorchen (*ought to in the nature of things*).
„Muß man hier Wein trinken?" – „Sie müssen nicht, aber Sie kön-
nen." (*You don't have to*).
Er muß es noch nicht wissen, sonst ... (*he cannot know it yet, other-
wise* ...).
Er muß hier gewesen sein (*must have been, no doubt he was here*).
Wir mußten gehorchen (*had to obey*).
Wir mußten lachen (*could not help laughing*).
Gerade *er* mußte kommen (*as bad luck would have it it was he who came*).
Diese Frage mußte kommen (*was bound to come*).
Sie mußte in der Nacht geschlafen haben (*must have slept, no doubt she
had slept*).
Man müßte sich erkundigen, um ... (*would have to inquire*).
Das **müßtest** du doch wissen (*you really ought to know that*).
Er **hat** gehorchen müssen (*he has had to, he had to obey*).
Er hätte das Haus nicht verlassen müssen (*should not have, for he need
not have*).
Beim ersten Anblick hätte es ihn verraten müssen (*could not have
failed to betray him*).

(f) **sollen** (soll, sollst, soll, sollen, etc.; sollte, etc.)

Er soll alles haben (*shall*). Du sollst nicht stehlen (*shalt*).
Was soll ich tun (*shall*)? Soll ich auch kommen (*shall*).
Sollen wir nach Hause gehen (*shall*, i.e. *oughtn't we perhaps to*)?
Ich soll hier bleiben (*am to, am supposed to, am expected to*).
Was soll ich tun (*what am I to do*)?
Was soll ich dir vorlesen (*what would you like me to read to you*)?
Du sollst da bleiben (*I want you to stay there*).
Er soll gleich kommen (*tell him to come at once*).
Er soll es tun (*make him do it*).
Was soll das (heißen) (*what is the meaning of that, e.g. behaviour*)?
Was soll man da sagen (*can*)?
Kinder sollen ihren Eltern gehorchen (*should = are expected to*).
Soll er so ins Haus fallen (*is it to be tolerated that*)?
Es soll zum Kloster gehören (*is said to belong*).
Es soll zum Kloster gehört haben (*is said to have belonged*).

Was sollte er anfangen (*was he to do*)?
Er sollte das erst später erfahren (*was to, was destined to*).
Es sollte zum Kloster gehört haben (*was said to have*).
Er sollte (*subj.*) eilen (*ought to*).
Sollte (*subj.*) das wahr sein (*can it be true*)?
Wenn er mich sehen sollte (*subj.*) (*were he to/should he*).
Sollte (*subj.*) er kommen, so ... (*were he to/should he*).
Wie hätte ich das ahnen sollen (*should I have suspected*)?
Er hätte das Haus nicht verlassen sollen (*should not have, ought not to have*, i.e. *it was his duty not to*).

(g) **wollen** (will, willst, will, wollen, etc.; wollte, etc.)

Er will alles sehen (*wants to*).
Willst du mitkommen (*will*)?
Er will heute früher nach Hause kommen (*intends, wants to*).
Er will durchaus, daß ich komme (*insists on my coming*).
Ich will ihn nicht beleidigen (*don't mean to*).
Er will nicht arbeiten (*will not, refuses to*).
Willst du Weißwein, oder willst du lieber Rotwein (*will you have . . . do you prefer*)?
Wollen wir ins Theater (gehen) (*shall we go*)?
Wir wollen ins Theater (gehen) (*let us go*)!
Wir wollen eben ausgehen (*are just going out*).
Die Arbeit will kein Ende nehmen (*shows no signs of*).
So etwas will gelernt sein (*needs to be*).
Er will alles besser wissen (*claims to know*).
Er will sie gesehen haben (*claims, asserts that*).
Ich will nichts gesagt haben (*I take back what I've said*).

Er wollte alles sehen (*wanted to, meant to, intended to*).
Er wollte nicht arbeiten (*would not, refused to*).
Die Sonne wollte eben untergehen (*was just about to*).
Er wollte sie gesehen haben (*claimed he had*).
Die Arbeit wollte kein Ende nehmen (*showed no signs of*).

Er hat nicht kommen wollen (*did not want to*).

Er hatte kommen wollen (*had intended to*).

Er hätte kommen wollen (*would have liked to*).

Er würde es schon tun wollen, wenn er nur könnte (*he would want to, like to*).

(h) Combinations of modals that are quite possible in English have sometimes to be rendered in other ways in German.

Er hätte das nicht einmal wollen können (R. HUCH).
Warum sollen wir das nicht auch dürfen (H. MANN).

But Er wird vielleicht früher abreisen müssen (*may have to*).
Er wird vielleicht früher abreisen wollen (*may want to*).
Du wirst doch kommen wollen (*you must want to come*)!

(i) The verb *gehen* or *fahren*, etc., is often understood but left unexpressed
with modals, e.g. Ich muß/soll/will jetzt nach Hause (gehen). Darf
ich jetzt nach Hause (gehen).

68 Lassen

(a) (= *leave*) Ich habe es zu Hause gelassen. Ich habe es auf dem Tisch
liegen lassen, in der Ecke stehen lassen. Laß mich allein!

(b) (= *make*) Er hat mich warten lassen. Er läßt seine Schüler zu viel
auswendig lernen. Das läßt mich glauben/annehmen/vermuten, daß ...

(c) (= *get s.b. to do s.th.*) Ich ließ die Kinder für mich abwaschen. Ich
ließ ihn es mir ausführlich erzählen. Ich ließ ihn den Plan ausführen.

(d) (= *get, have s.th. done (for oneself)*) Ich ließ es sofort bringen. Ich habe
mir die Haare schneiden lassen, mir einen Anzug machen lassen.

(e) (= *let*) Laß mich kommen! Das läßt mich hoffen, daß er ... Er ließ
sie nicht gehen, ohne ...

(f) (= *can be*) Das läßt sich nur schwer sagen. Das läßt sich nicht leugnen
(*denied*).

(g) (*Idioms*) Er hat ihn kommen lassen (*sent for him*). Er läßt Ihnen sagen,
daß ... (*he wants me to tell you that ...*). Das lasse ich mir nicht
gefallen (*I'll not put up with that*). Er läßt deine Mutter (herzlich)
grüßen (*he sends his (kindest) regards to your mother*). Wir wollen es
dabei lassen (*we'll leave it at that*).

69 The Passive Voice

(a) Er wird getragen (*is carried, is being carried*), wurde getragen (*was carried, was being carried*), ist getragen worden (*has been carried*), war
getragen worden (*had been carried*), wird getragen werden (*will be
carried*), sei gegrüßt/umarmt! (*hail!/a hug!*) – the passive imperative is
restricted to one or two expressions only).

(b) Es muß aufgegessen werden (*must be eaten up*), mußte aufgegessen
werden (*had to be*), hat aufgegessen werden müssen (*has had to be*),

hätte aufgegessen werden müssen (*should have been*), wird aufgegessen werden müssen (*will have to be*).

Es muß (mußte) aufgegessen **worden** sein (*must have been eaten up*); damit wir gerettet werden könnten (*so that we could be rescued*); sie hätten nicht geschrieben zu werden brauchen (*might as well have not been written*, i.e. *for all the use* ...).

(c) *By* is translated by *von* (agent), *durch* (means), *mit* (instrument).

Die Tür wurde **von** einem Diener geöffnet.
Durch seine Hilfe wurde es möglich gemacht.
Er wurde **mit** einem Messer erstochen (*stabbed*).

(d) The subject of the passive is the direct object of the active. Indirect objects remain indirect in the passive.

Er wurde freigelassen.
Ihm wurde **ein schöner Wagen** gegeben (*he was given a* ...).
Er wurde seines Amtes enthoben (*he was removed from* ...).

(e) An impersonal passive construction (introduced by *es* – in the main, but never in the subordinate clause – only if this is the first word) has to be used when the verb is intransitive.

Es wurde lange getanzt *or* Lange wurde getanzt (*dancing went on for a long time*).
But Obgleich lange getanzt wurde, ...
Mir wurde versichert, daß ... (*I was assured* ...).
Ihnen muß beigebracht werden, wie ... (*they must be taught how*).
An Ihrem Mut ist nie gezweifelt worden (*your courage has never been doubted*).

(f) The infinitive + *zu* preceded by *sein, bleiben, stehen* and, without *zu*, *lassen* (with reflexive verb) has modal and passive force.

Das ist leicht zu erraten (*can easily be guessed, is easy to guess*).
Nichts war zu finden (*nothing could be, was to be found*).
Das Haus ist zu vermieten (*to (be) let*). Dem ist nicht zu helfen.
Der Erfolg bleibt abzuwarten (*remains to be seen*).
Das steht zu erwarten (*is to be expected*).
Diese Beispiele ließen sich leicht vervielfachen (*could easily be multiplied*).
Das läßt sich leicht sagen (*is easily said*).
Sie ließen sich hineinziehen (*let themselves be drawn in*).

(g) The statal passive (*sein* + past participle) must be distinguished from the actional passive (*werden* + past participle). Compare:

Die Tür **war** schon geschlossen (*was already shut*).
Die Tür **wurde** eben geschlossen (*was just being shut*), **wurde** jeden Abend um 6 Uhr geschlossen (i.e. *habitually*).

Note the following common statal passives:

Er war entschlossen/geneigt/gezwungen, es zu tun (*resolved/inclined/ compelled*); es war gefüllt/erfüllt mit/von (*filled with*), versehen mit (*provided with*); es war durchdrungen von (*filled with, steeped in*), umgeben von/mit (*surrounded by/with*); sie war in Weiß gekleidet (*dressed in*), in einen dicken Mantel eingehüllt (*wrapped in*).

(h) Note the following alternative ways of expressing the English passive:

i By reflexive verbs: sich befassen mit (*be concerned with*); sich erheben (*be raised*); sich erneuen (*be renewed*); sich (er)öffen (*be opened*); sich spiegeln (*be mirrored*); sich verdichten (*be consolidated*). Es stellte sich heraus, daß sie ... enthielt (*it was found to contain*).

ii By a verb in the active: entstammen (*be derived*); erlöschen (*be extinguished*); erschrecken (*be frightened*); ertrinken (*be drowned*); fußen auf (*be founded on*); heißen (*be called*); ruhen auf (*be based on*); er hatte es ihr angetan (*she was fascinated by him*); sie pflegten zu sagen (*were accustomed to*); er trug einen Anzug (*was dressed in*); sie stimmten darin überein, daß ... (*it was agreed among them that ...*); er geriet in Versuchung (*was tempted*).

iii By *dürfen, sollen, lassen*: er darf es tun (*is allowed to*); er soll es getan haben (*is said to*); mit denen es sich befassen soll (*which it is called upon to deal with*); er sollte sich einmischen (*was expected to*); es sollte ausdrücken (*was meant to*); ich würde sie nicht ertränken lassen (*would not have them, cause them to be, drowned*).

iv By *man*: man fragte ihn (*he was asked*); man hat es erreicht (*it was reached*); sie erwarten, daß man sie verschönert (*they expect to be idealised*); ... das man nennen könnte (*that could be called*).

v By constructions like: es heißt (*we are told*); er zeigte sich wohl überlegen (*he may be said to have shown himself superior*); etwas anderes ist notwendig (*is needed*), ist erforderlich (*is required*).

vi By a present participle construction (cf. *64(d)*): ein nie zu vergessendes Erlebnis (*an experience never to be forgotten*).

70 The Formation of the Subjunctive

(a) The endings of the present and imperfect subjunctive are the same for all verbs, except the 1st and 3rd sing. pres. of *sein*.

-e, -est, -e, -en, -et, -en.

(b) The present subjunctive (nowadays, however, used only in the third person singular except in the case of *sein* and the first person singular of the modal auxiliaries) is formed by adding these endings to the stem of the infinitive:

er sag-**e** er geh-**e,** er hab-**e,** er werd-**e,** ich/er könn-**e.**
But ich sei, du sei(**e**)**st**, er sei, wir sei**en**, ihr sei**et** (*rarely used*), sie (Sie) sei**en**.

(c) The imperfect subjunctive is formed by adding these endings to the past stem of weak and strong verbs. Strong verbs modify the stem vowel if possible, as do also *haben*, *wissen* and *werden*.

ich macht-**e**, er ging-**e**, ihr gäb-**et**, sie wär-**en**; er hätt-**e**, ich wüßt-**e**, sie würd-**en**.

(d) The perfect and pluperfect subjunctive are formed by the present and imperfect subjunctive of *haben* or *sein* together with the past participle. The perfect subjunctive when conjugated with *haben* is now only used in the third person singular.

er habe gesagt, er habe gegeben, ich sei gekommen; ich hätte gesagt, wir hätten gegeben, sie wären gekommen.

(e) Some verbs have older alternative forms of the imperfect subjunctive; *sterben*, *verderben*, *werben* and *werfen* have no alternative modern forms.

beföhle, begönne, empföhle, hülfe, schölte, schwömme, spönne; stürbe, verdürbe, würbe, würfe:

(f) Imperfect subjunctive of irregular weak verbs:

brennte, kennte, nennte, rennte, sendete, wendete and their compounds; brächte, dächte and their compounds; sollte, wollte.

71 The Subjunctive in Indirect Speech

(a) In turning direct speech – statements and questions – into indirect speech the following changes in the mood and tense of the verbs take place:

DIRECT SPEECH			INDIRECT SPEECH
Present Indicative		becomes	Present (or Imperfect) Subjunctive
Imperfect Indicative ⎫ Perfect Indicative ⎬ (= Past) Pluperfect Indicative ⎭		become	Perfect (or Pluperfect) Subjunctive
Future Indicative ⎫ (= Future) Conditional ⎭		become	Future Subjunctive or Conditional

i Er sagt, sie sei (wäre) unglücklich (*she is*), sie sei (wäre) unglücklich gewesen (*has been, was*), sie wolle (wollte) kommen (*wants*), sie habe (hätte) immer kommen wollen (*wanted, has wanted, had wanted*), sie habe (hätte) nicht geschlafen (*has not slept, did not sleep*), sie komme (käme) erst später (*is coming, will be coming*).

Er sagte, sie sei (wäre) sehr unglücklich (*she was*), sie wolle (wollte) kommen (*wanted*), sie habe (hätte) nicht geschlafen (*had not slept*), sie komme (käme) erst später (*was coming, i.e. would be coming*).

Er sagte,	wenn sie sofort komme (käme), tue (täte) er es.
Er sagte,	es sei die Tochter der Frau, bei der ... er wohne (ANDERSCH).
Er sagte, daß	sie sehr unglücklich sei (wäre), daß sie nicht kommen wolle (wollte), etc.

ii Er fragte sie, ob sie Zeit habe (hätte) (*if she had*), ob sie gut ge-schlafen habe (hätte) (*had slept*), wann sie kommen könne (könnte) (*could come*), wann sie komme (käme) (*was coming*, i.e. *would be coming*).

Er fragte, was der Mann wolle, der eben gekommen sei.

iii Er sagte ihr, sie solle (sollte) sofort kommen (*told her to come*), sie möchte alles liegen lassen (*told her to leave everything*).

(b) If in indirect speech the present, perfect or future subjunctive forms are indistinguishable from the corresponding indicative forms, the im-perfect subjunctive, pluperfect subjunctive or conditional **must** be used. Otherwise, modern usage tends to prefer the pluperfect subjunctive and conditional, but, except in N. Germany, not the imperfect subjunctive. In any case, all possible consistency in the use of tenses should be aimed at.

Er sagte mir, sie machten (*not* machen) alles verkehrt, sie hätten (*not* haben) alles verkehrt gemacht, sie würden (*not* werden) alles verkehrt machen, sie würden bald gehen (*not* sie gehen *or* gingen) (*were going*, i.e. *would be going*).

(c) In a passage of indirect speech *daß* is usually omitted.

(d) The subjunctive does not necessarily have to be used in indirect speech. It is normally used in indirect speech either (i) when the writer does not wish to vouch for the truth of what is reported or (ii) when he wishes to convey that what is reported is not true or that he does not agree with it. If on the other hand the writer is certain of his facts and wishes to convey this certainty he will use the indicative. Compare the following examples taken from modern German authors:

Ich sage immer, daß ich nichts davon weiß (= *what I in fact always say*).

Ich sage, ich hätte mich verlaufen (= *I'll say what is not true*).

Ich glaube, sie ist schon zu Hause.

Ich glaube fast, daß Sie der Mann wären, mich zu verstehen.

Ich habe schon geglaubt, du seist nach Hause gegangen (*but now I see I am wrong*).

Sie können nicht wissen, wie meine Worte gemeint sind (*but I know*).

Ohne recht zu wissen, wo er sei ...

Plötzlich wußte ich, wer Sie sind.

Sie wußte, sie könne mir nicht helfen.

Er vermutete, daß es sie war.

72 Conditional Sentences and the Use of the Subjunctive

(a) **Indicative** in both clauses

Wenn ich Zeit habe, hole ich dich ab (*if I have time I'll fetch you*).
Wenn du Arbeit willst, können wir zu meinen Leuten fahren.
Ich komme am Montag, wenn ich es einrichten kann.
Ich werde es tun, wenn ich es einrichten kann.

(b) **Conditional** (*or* **subjunctive**) in the **main** clause, **subjunctive** in **subordinate** clause

Wenn ich Zeit hätte, würde ich dich abholen (*or* holte ich dich ab) (*if I had time I would fetch you*).
Wenn er kommen sollte, würden wir uns freuen (*if he were to*).
Wenn du Arbeit wolltest, könnten wir zu meinen Leuten fahren.
Ich würde am Montag kommen (*or* ich käme am Montag), wenn ich es einrichten könnte.

NOTE: The conditional in the subordinate clause, though met with in good authors and though very common in colloquial German is apt to be stylistically clumsy and should be used with discretion in German prose composition, restricted rather to the conversational passages.

Wenn sie ihn lieben würde, würde sie es sofort sagen (MUSIL).
Wenn sie eine Möglichkeit finden würde, ... (KAFKA).
Wenn du sie kennen würdest, dann wüßtest du, daß ... (RINSER).

(c) **Subjunctive** in **both** clauses

Wenn ich Zeit gehabt hätte, hätte ich dich abgeholt (*if I had had time I would have fetched you*).
Wenn du Arbeit gewollt hättest, hätten wir zu meinen Leuten fahren können.
Ich wäre am Montag gekommen, wenn ich es hätte einrichten können (*if I could have managed it*).

(d) **Omission of** *wenn*

Kommt er, so/dann können wir die Sache besprechen (*if he comes*).
Käme er bald (*or* sollte er bald kommen), so würden wir uns sehr freuen (*were he to*).
Wäre er gekommen, so hätten wir uns gefreut (*had he come*).
Hätte ich das Große Los gewonnen, so ... (*had I won*).

(e) Since *wenn* with the present indicative may also mean 'when' or 'whenever' *falls* ('in case', 'if') or *sollte* should be used when ambiguity must be avoided.

Falls er anruft, sag ihm ... **Sollte** er anrufen, so ...

(f) When either of the clauses states a fact the indicative must be used in both clauses.

> Wenn er böse war, so waren wir es noch viel mehr (*if he was angry we were much more so*).
>
> Wenn ihn der Bruder für einen Dieb hielt, so konnte ja jeder Fremde dasselbe oder Besseres leisten als er (SCHNITZLER).
>
> Wenn seine Hand gezittert hat und er nicht völlig Herr seiner selbst war, so geschah es, weil ... (T. MANN).

73 Other Uses of the Subjunctive

(a) In main clauses:

i Man nehme ein Pfund Butter! Es lebe die Freiheit!
Gehen wir! Es koste, was es wolle.
Möge Gott mich totschlagen!

ii Käme er doch bald (*if only he would come soon*)!
Hätte ich nur fleißiger gearbeitet!
Beinahe hätte ich dich nicht erkannt (*I nearly didn't recognise you*).
Er wäre beinahe/fast gestorben (*he almost died*).

iii Nun wären wir zu Hause (*well, home at last*)!
Wäre das möglich (*is it really possible*)?

(b) In subordinate clauses:

i Purpose:

> Er wollte, daß wir sofort kämen (*wanted us to*).
> Ich wünschte, ich könnte (*I wish I could*).
> Sie möchte, daß ich die Sirenen und die Flieger ganz vergäße (LEFORT)
> Er wartete, daß sie käme (*for her to come*).
> *But* Er **will**, daß sie sofort **kommt.**
> Er tat alles, damit seine Familie zu essen hätte/hatte.
> *But* Er **tut** alles, damit seine Familie zu essen **hat.**

ii Negation, restriction or denial:

> Ich kenne niemand, der so dumm wäre (*who is*).
> Niemand, der mein wächsernes Gesicht gewärmt hätte (*who warmed, nobody to warm*)! (AICHINGER)
> Ein Orchester, das nur aus Pauken, Trommeln, Kastagnetten und Schlag- und Geräuschinstrumenten bestände, wäre ein Unmögliches (W. SCHNEIDER).
> Nicht daß er ein Musterschüler geworden wäre (*has become*).
> Er leugnete ab, daß es so etwas überhaupt gäbe.
> Die Entfernung war zu groß, als daß er das Haus hätte erkennen können (*for him to be able to*) (ANDERSCH).
> Kein Tag verging, ohne daß ich daran gedacht hätte/hatte (*without my thinking of it*).

D

But Kein Tag vergeht, ohne daß er daran **denkt**.

Anstatt daß er zu ihnen gegangen wäre/war, mußte seine Mutter zu ihnen gehen (*instead of his going*).

But Anstatt daß er zu ihnen **geht**, muß seine Mutter zu ihnen gehen.

iii Er sieht aus, als ob er krank sei/wäre, als sei/wäre er krank (*he looks as if he is/were ill*).

Er tat (so), als ob er schliefe (*pretended to be asleep*).

NOTE: The *als ob/als* construction can only be used with a finite verb. With the participles and the infinitive *wie* is used:

Es sah aus wie aus Gold gemacht (*as if made of*).
Er lachte wie verrückt (*as if mad, like one mad*).
Er streckte die Hand aus, wie um sie zu liebkosen (*as though to caress her*).

74 Verbs governing the Dative

WEAK

angehören *belong to (s.th)*
antworten *answer (s.b.)*
*begegnen *meet*
beiwohnen *attend, be present at*
danken *thank*
dienen *serve*
drohen *threaten*
*entstammen *be derived from*
fehlen *be missing; be wrong with*
(*)folgen *follow; obey*
gehorchen *obey*
gehören *belong to (s.b.)*
genügen *suffice*
glauben *believe (s.b.)*
gratulieren *congratulate*
imponieren *impress*
mißtrauen *mistrust*
sich nähern *approach*
nützen *be of use to*
passen *suit*
*passieren *happen to*
schaden *harm*
schmecken *like (taste of)*
schmeicheln *flatter*
trotzen *defy*
vertrauen *trust*
sich widmen *devote o.s. to*
zuhören *listen to*
zulächeln *smile at*

STRONG (see *102*)

*auffallen *strike one's attention, notice*
*einfallen *occur to*
*entfliehen *escape from*
*entgehen *elude, avoid, escape from*
*entkommen *get away, escape (from)*
entsprechen *suit, correspond to*
*entspringen *arise, proceed from, be an outcome of*
*erliegen *succumb to*
gefallen *please, like*
*gelingen *succeed, manage*
gelten *be intended for, matter to*
*geschehen *happen to*
gleichen *resemble*
helfen *help*
leid tun *be sorry (for)*
*mißlingen *fail*
*nachlaufen *run after*
nachsehen *follow with one's eyes*
*vorangehen *precede, go on ahead*
*vorausgehen *precede, go on ahead*
*vorkommen *seem to; (refl.) feel, think o.s.*
*weichen *yield to*
weh tun *hurt, ache*
widersprechen *contradict*
widerstehen *resist*
zusehen *watch*
*zustoßen *befall, happen to*

Ich gratuliere Ihnen. Es gelang mir, der Gefahr zu entkommen. Er tut mir leid (*I am sorry for him*). Es wird Ihnen dort gefallen (*you'll like it there*). Das kommt mir komisch vor (*it seems odd to me*). Ich kam mir dumm vor (*I felt stupid*).

75 Verbs governing the Accusative and Dative

WEAK
anvertrauen *entrust*
auferlegen *impose, inflict on*
beibringen (*irr.*) *teach*
berichten *report*
besorgen *get s.th. for s.b.*
bringen (*irr.*) *bring, take*
einbringen (*irr.*) *bring in, yield*
einflößen *inspire with*
einräumen *concede, give up to*
einschärfen *impress/inculcate on*
erklären *explain; declare*
erlauben *allow, permit*
ersparen *save s.b. s.th.*
erzählen *tell, relate*
gewähren *grant, accord*
gönnen *not begrudge*
hinzufügen *add*
klagen *complain of*
liefern *deliver, furnish, supply*
melden *announce*
mitteilen *impart, inform of*
reichen *hand, pass, reach*
sagen *say, tell*
schenken *give, present*
schicken *send*
senden (*irr.*) *send*
verdanken *owe to*
verkaufen *sell*
verschaffen *get, procure for*
verweigern *refuse s.b. s.th.*
vorspielen *play to*
vorstellen *introduce*
wünschen *wish*
zahlen *pay*
zeigen *show, point out*
zumuten *expect of, demand of*

STRONG (see *102*)
anbieten *offer*
aufgeben *assign, set* (e.g. *a task*)
befehlen *order*
beschreiben *describe*
beweisen *prove*
bieten *bid, offer*
empfehlen *recommend*
entreißen *seize from*
entziehen *deprive of, withdraw from*
geben *give*
gebieten *command*
hinterlassen *bequeath*
leihen *lend*
nachsehen *overlook* (e.g. *fault*)
raten *advise*
schreiben *write*
überlassen *leave to* (*s.b. else*)
verbergen *conceal from*
verbieten *forbid*
vergeben *forgive*
verleihen *grant, bestow on, confer, endow with*
verraten *betray*
verschreiben *prescribe* (e.g. *medicine*)
versprechen *promise*
verzeihen *pardon*
vorenthalten *withhold from*
vorlesen *read aloud*
vorschlagen *suggest*
vorwerfen *reproach with*
vorziehen *prefer*
weisen *show*
zurückgeben *return*
zurufen *call out to*
es einem antun *fascinate s.b.*

Er flößte ihnen Mut ein. Das kann ich ihnen nicht zumuten. Das verdanke ich Ihnen allein.

76 Verbs governing the Genitive

WEAK

sich bedienen *use*
bedürfen *(irr.) need*
sich bemächtigen *seize, take possession of, usurp*
sich entledigen *get rid of, acquit o.s. of, fulfil*
sich erbarmen *have mercy on, take pity on*
sich erfreuen *enjoy*
sich erinnern *remember*
sich erwehren *restrain, ward off*
gedenken *(irr.) bear in mind, remember*
sich rühmen *boast of*
sich schämen *be ashamed of*
sich vergewissern *assure o.s. of*
sich versichern *assure o.s. of*

STRONG (see 102)

sich annehmen *take charge, care of*
sich begeben *waive, renounce*
sich enthalten *refrain, abstain from*
entraten *dispense with*
sich entschlagen *part with, get rid of*
sich entsinnen *remember*
sich verschließen *shut one's eyes to*
sich versehen *expect s.th. confidently*

Es bedurfte nur eines Wortes. Er konnte sich des Lachens nicht enthalten Er rühmte sich dessen, niemals zu spät gekommen zu sein.

77 Verbs governing the Accusative and Genitive

WEAK

anklagen *accuse of*
berauben *rob of*
beschuldigen *accuse of*
bezichtigen *accuse of*
entkleiden *deprive of, strip*
entwöhnen *break of (habit)*
verdächtigen *suspect of*
würdigen *deem worthy of*

STRONG (see 102)

entbinden *release, absolve from* (e.g. *duty*)
entheben *remove from, relieve of* (e.g. *office*)
zeihen *accuse of*

Sie wollte mich keines Blickes würdigen. Er wurde seines Amtes enthoben.

78 Verbs governing a Double Accusative

WEAK

kosten *cost*
lehren *teach*
nennen *(irr.) call, name*

STRONG (see 102)

heißen *call*
schelten *call s.b. (s.th. derogatory)*

79 Verbs followed by a Prepositional Object

(a) General remarks:

i   Many verbs take a prepositional object, i.e. a noun or pronoun preceded by a preposition or adverbial compound:

Ich verlasse mich auf meinen Freund, auf ihn.
Ich verlasse mich auf mein Glück, darauf (*rely on it*).

ii The prepositional object of a number of such verbs can be a clause or an infinitive phrase. Such clauses or infinitive phrases are normally preceded by the appropriate adverbial compound – *daran, darauf, damit*, etc. If two persons are involved a clause must be used introduced by *daß* or an interrogative; otherwise an infinitive construction is possible and usually preferable. The English translation is often a gerund. (But see *48(f) vi* for construction with relative clauses).

Ich verlasse mich darauf, daß du kommst (*I rely on your coming*).
Sie erinnerte sich daran, wie er ausgesehen hatte.
Es hängt davon ab, wann Sie abreisen wollen.
Ich denke nicht daran, mich darüber zu beklagen (*of complaining*).

iii Those verbs in the following lists that are capable of the above construction (ii) are marked by a dagger †.

iv Some of the nouns and adjectives listed in *56* as well as a few other expressions are also capable of this construction. See *(v)* below.

WEAK

STRONG (see *102*)

(b) **an + accusative**

†denken (*irr.*) *think of*	binden *tie to*
†erinnern *remind*	*festbinden *tie up, tether to*
†sich erinnern *remember*	†*gehen *proceed to*
†gewöhnen *accustom to*	sich halten *stick, adhere to* (e.g.
†sich gewöhnen *get used to*	rules)
†glauben *believe in*	*herangehen *go up to, tackle* (e.g.
sich klammern *cling to, clutch at*	problem)
sich lehnen *lean against*	*herankommen *come up to*
†sich machen *proceed to*	schreiben *write to*
stecken *pin to*	verraten *betray to*
sich wenden (*irr.*) *turn, apply to*	verweisen *refer s.b. to s.b.*

Er verriet ihn an seine Feinde. Er hat sich daran gewöhnt, ohne Schlafmittel zu schlafen.

(c) **an + dative**

arbeiten *work at*	abnehmen *decrease in*
sich beteiligen *take part in*	gewinnen *gain in*
†erkennen (*irr.*) *recognise by*	hängen *care about, be attached to*

WEAK	STRONG (see 102)
*erkranken *be taken ill with*	leiden *suffer from, be liable to*
fehlen *be lacking in*	liegen *rest with, be up to; be one's*
sich freuen *take pleasure in*	*fault; matter to; be due to*
†hindern *prevent from*	*sterben *die of (illness)*
sich orientieren *take one's bearings*	teilnehmen *partake of,*
by	*participate in*
sich rächen *avenge o.s. on*	tragen *be weighed down by* (e.g. *guilt*)
teilhaben (*irr.*) *participate in*	verlieren *lose in*
†verhindern *prevent from*	* vorbeigehen *go past*
sich versuchen *try one's hand at*	* vorbeikommen *come, get past*
sich versündigen *sin against*	* vorbeilaufen *run past*
verzweifeln *despair of*	ziehen *pull on, at*
sich weiden *feast one's eyes on*	zunehmen *increase in*
zweifeln *doubt*	

Es fehlt ihm an Mut. Er hinderte sie daran, mit seinem Freund zu sprechen. Es liegt an mir, ob er kommt oder nicht (*it rests with me, it's up to me, whether* . . .). Mir liegt viel/wenig/nichts daran (*it matters much* . . .).

(d) auf + accusative

†achten *heed, look after*	es abgesehen haben *have designs on*
†anspielen *allude to*	†*ankommen *depend on,*
antworten *answer s.th.*	*be concerned to*
anwenden (*irr.*) *apply s.th. to s.th.*	es darauf ankommen lassen *risk,*
sich aufbauen *be based/founded on*	*chance it*
†aufmerksam machen *call attention*	†*ausgehen *be bent on*
to	†*aussein *be out for s.th.*
aufpassen *keep an eye on*	sich belaufen *amount to* (e.g. *bills*)
beschränken *limit, confine to,*	sich besinnen *remember*
cut down to	sich beziehen *refer to*
blicken *look, gaze at*	†dringen *press for s.th.*
fluchen *swear at*	*eingehen *agree to; go into details*
*folgen *follow upon*	sich einlassen *let o.s get involved in*
sich freuen *look forward to*	*gehen *look out on to*
sich gründen *be based on*	*hinauslaufen *amount,*
hinarbeiten *work for (an object)*	*be tantamount to*
†hindeuten *indicate, intimate*	†hinweisen *point, refer to, indicate*
†hoffen *hope for*	*kommen *hit upon*
hören *listen, pay attention to*	schießen *shoot at*
*klettern *climb up* (e.g. *tree*)	sehen *look, glance at*
sich konzentrieren *concentrate on,*	sinnen *scheme, plot s.th.*
centre on	*stoßen *come upon, run into s.b.*
passen *watch for, fit (on, into)*	trinken *drink to, toast*
†rechnen *count on*	†sich verlassen *rely on*
trauen *trust in*	verschieben *postpone to*

WEAK	STRONG (see *102*)
vertrauen *trust in*	sich verstehen *be skilled in,*
verwenden *apply s.th. to,*	*expert at*
bring to bear on	verweisen *refer s.b. to s.th.*
†verzichten *do without, renounce*	weisen *point to, at*
†sich vorbereiten *prepare for*	*zugehen *go up to*
warten *wait for*	*zukommen *come up to*
zeigen *point to, at*	*zulaufen *run up to*
†zurückführen *attribute,*	zutreffen *apply to, be true of*
trace back to	

Alles ist auf seinen Mangel an Mut zurückzuführen. Er machte mich darauf aufmerksam. Es läuft auf dasselbe hinaus. Es kommt darauf an, wie man es versteht (*it depends on the way*). Ihnen kam es darauf an, zu gewinnen (*they were concerned to*).

(e) auf + dative

†beharren, *stick, adhere to*	†bestehen *insist on*
(e.g. *opinion*)	
beruhen *be based on, rest on*	
fußen *be founded on*	

Das beruht auf einem Irrtum. Er besteht darauf, daß wir kommen.

(f) aus + dative

erhellen *be evident from*	bestehen *consist of*
†*folgen *follow from*	*entkommen *escape out of*
†folgern *infer from*	*entspringen *escape out of*
lernen *learn from*	*entstehen *originate in, arise*
machen *make s.th. of/from*	†sich ergeben *result, follow from*
resultieren *result from*	†ersehen *see from*
übersetzen *translate from*	†schließen *conclude from*
	*werden *become of*

Der Verbrecher entsprang aus dem Zug, aus dem Gefängnis. Daraus ergibt sich, daß kein wahres Wort daran ist.

(g) bei + dative

sich bedanken *thank*	*bleiben *stay with; stick to*
†beharren *stick to* (e.g. *opinion*)	ergreifen *seize by* (e.g. *hand*)
sich beklagen *complain to*	halten *hold by* (e.g. *hand*)
sich entschuldigen *apologise to*	helfen *help with*
hindern *obstruct*	nehmen *take* (e.g. *by hand*)
wohnen *live with*	vorsprechen *call on*

Er bedankte sich bei mir. Er half uns bei der Arbeit. Sie hielt ihn bei der Hand.

WEAK

(h) für + accusative

bestimmen *destine, mean for*
†danken *thank for*
sich einsetzen *champion s.th./s.b.*
sich interessieren *be interested in*
kämpfen *fight for*
schwärmen *enthuse about*
†sorgen *see to, look after*
stimmen *vote for*

STRONG (see *102*)

†*eintreten *plead for s.th./s.b.*
†sich entscheiden *decide for, in favour of*
†gelten *be considered; be true for*
halten *consider, deem, think, take for/to be*
nehmen *take*
zutreffen *be true of*

Nimm es nicht für ungut (*don't take it amiss*)! Er interessiert sich für alles. Er sorgte dafür, daß die Kinder gut erzogen wurden.

(i) gegen + accusative

†einwenden *object to, have objection to*
†etwas/nichts haben *have some/no objection to*
kämpfen *fight against*
†protestieren *protest against*
stimmen *vote against*
sich sträuben *boggle at, oppose*
sich wehren *oppose*

abstechen *stand out clearly against*
sich aussprechen *make objections to s.th.*
*einschreiten *take action against*
†sich entscheiden *decide against*
sich erheben *rise up against*
†sprechen *speak against*
verstoßen *offend against*

Was haben Sie dagegen? Ich habe nichts dagegen. Er wendete dagegen ein, daß er an dem Tag nicht frei war.

(j) in + accusative

sich einmischen *interfere in, mix o.s. up in*
einweihen *initiate into*
einwilligen *consent, agree to*
sich fügen *acquiesce in, submit to*
(sich) kleiden *dress (o.s.) in*
sich mischen *interfere in*
übersetzen *translate into*
sich verlieben *fall in love with*
versetzen *place in(to)*
verwandeln *transform, change into*
sich verwandeln *turn, be transformed into*
verwickeln *involve in*
sich verwickeln *be involved in*

*ausbrechen *burst out into*
dringen *urge upon, press s.b.*
*einbiegen *turn into (e.g. road)*
*einbrechen *break into, burgle*
*eindringen *force one's way in*
*einfallen *invade*
einlassen *let s.b./s.th. in(to)*
sich einlassen *let o.s get involved in*
einschließen *confine within, shut in*
*einsteigen *mount, get in, board (vehicle)*
*eintreten *enter*
sich ergeben *resign o.s. to*
*geraten *get into (e.g. difficulties)*

Er übersetzte das Buch aus dem Englischen ins Deutsche. Er hat sich ins Unvermeidliche fügen müssen.

WEAK   STRONG (see *102*)

(k) in + dative

sich irren *be mistaken, wrong about*	*ankommen *arrive at, in*
*einkehren *put up (at inn)*	†bestehen *consist in*
sich spiegeln *be mirrored in*	*erscheinen *appear at, in*
†übereinstimmen *agree about, in*	†liegen *reside/consist in*
	sich verfangen *catch* (intr.) *in*
	*verschwinden *disappear in*

Ihr Fingernagel verfing sich in ihrem Kleid. Wir stimmten darin überein, daß Karl fort mußte (*we agreed that*).

(l) mit + dative

aufhören *stop s.th.*	†sich abfinden *accept, acquiesce in, compound with*
sich befassen *deal, be concerned with, handle*	†anfangen *begin by*
†sich beschäftigen *occupy o.s. with*	†beginnen *begin by*
handeln *trade in*	fortfahren *go on with, continue*
nicken *nod (the head)*	*geschehen *happen to*
prahlen *boast of*	sprechen *speak to, with*
†rechnen *count on, expect*	*umgehen *handle, entertain* (e.g. idea), *associate with*
übereinstimmen *agree with s.b., square with s.th.*	verbinden *connect, join*
†verbringen (*irr.*) *spend (doing s.th.)*	versehen *provide with*
sich verschmelzen *melt into*	*zusammenstoßen *collide with*
verwechseln *confuse with*	
wedeln *wag*	
winken *wave, beckon*	
†zubringen (*irr.*) *spend (doing s.th.)*	

Das stimmt nicht damit überein. Sie winkte mit der Hand. Du mußt dich damit abfinden, daß es nicht anders geht.

(m) nach + dative

*abreisen *set off for*	aussehen *look like*
angeln *fish for*	graben *dig for*
†sich erkundigen *enquire about s.b.*	greifen *clutch at, catch hold of*
forschen *search after*	riechen *smell of*
†fragen *enquire about s.b./s.th.*	schreien *shout for*
schicken *send for*	sehen *look after*
schmecken *taste of*	sich umsehen *look round for*
†sich sehnen *long for*	
streben *strive after /for*	
suchen *search for*	
†urteilen *judge by*	

Sie schickte nach dem Arzt. Er konnte nur nach dem urteilen, was er gesehen hatte. Ich sehne mich danach, ins Bett zu gehen.

WEAK STRONG (see *102*)

(n) **über + accusative**

†sich beklagen *complain of*
†berichten *report, impart*
†*erstaunen *be surprised at*
†sich freuen *be glad about,*
    pleased with
sich hermachen *fall upon, attack*
herrschen *rule over*
†klagen *complain of* ·
†lachen *laugh at, about*
†nachdenken *think about, of, over*
†reden *talk about*
regieren *govern*
†schimpfen *grumble about*
†spotten *mock at, deride*
sich täuschen *be mistaken about*
urteilen *pass judgment on, judge*
verfügen *possess, have at one's*
    disposal
wachen *watch over*
weinen *weep over, about*
†sich wundern *be surprised at*

sich aussprechen *discuss*
†beraten *give advice about*
entscheiden *decide upon*
erfahren *learn about, of*
gebieten *have control over, have*
    at one's command
*gehen *exceed, surpass* (e.g.
    expectations)
*kommen *fall on, overwhelm*
lesen *lecture on*
†schreiben *write about*
sinnen *meditate, reflect (up)on*
†sprechen *speak about s.th.*
streiten *argue, dispute about*
sich streiten *quarrel about*
† sich unterhalten *converse about*

Er verfügt über überraschende Eigenschaften. Er beklagte sich darüber, daß sie nicht gekommen war.

(o) **um + accusative**

sich bemühen *try to help*
†beneiden *envy*
bringen (*irr.*) *deprive of, cheat out*
    of
†sich drehen *turn, hinge on*
flehen *implore for*
fragen *ask for* (e.g. *advice*)
†sich handeln *be a question,*
    matter of
kämpfen *fight, struggle for*
sich (be-)kümmern *concern o.s.,*
    worry about

sich bewerben *apply for* (e.g. *post*)
†bitten *ask for*
*gehen, *be a matter of, be at*
    stake
*herumkommen *get round* (e.g.
    difficulty)
*kommen *lose*
ringen *struggle for*
streiten *contend with s.b. for*
wissen *know about*

Er beneidet seinen Bruder um seinen Reichtum. Darum können wir nicht herumkommen. Es handelt sich darum, ob er noch lebt.

(p) **unter + accusative**

gehören *fall under, pertain to*
    *geraten *fall among, in with*

Das gehört unter diese Rubrik. Er geriet unter Räuber.

WEAK

(q) unter + dative

STRONG (see *102*)

†leiden *suffer emotionally under, in consequence of*

Er litt darunter, daß man nicht mit ihm verkehren wollte.

(r) von + dative

benachrichtigen *inform of*
denken (*irr.*) *think* (e.g. *well*) *of*
sich erholen *recover from*
†erzählen *relate about*
heilen *cure of*
leben *live on*
sagen *tell about*
†träumen *dream of*
überzeugen *convince of*
wimmeln *teem with*
wissen (*irr.*) *know about*

†abhalten *prevent, keep from*
†abhängen *depend on*
sich abheben *be silhouetted/ outlined, stand out against*
abziehen *deduct from*
gelten *be true of*
halten *think* (e.g. *well*) *of*
lossprechen *acquit of, absolve from*
†sprechen *speak of*
verstehen *know, understand about*
*weichen *budge from*

Was hielt ihn davon ab? Wovon lebt er?

(s) vor + dative

†Angst haben *be afraid of*
†bewahren *preserve from*
†sich fürchten *be afraid of*
†sich hüten *beware of*
schützen *protect from*
verstecken *hide from*
†warnen *warn against*
weinen *weep* (e.g. *for joy*)

†*erschrecken *be startled at*
*fliehen *flee from*
sich in acht nehmen, *be careful of, mind*
*sterben *die* (e.g. *of boredom*)
verbergen *conceal from*
*weichen *give way to*

Nimm dich in acht davor! Hüten Sie sich (davor), es ihm zu sagen!

(t) wegen + genitive

loben *praise for*
sich schämen *be ashamed because of*
tadeln *blame for*

schelten *scold, rebuke for*

Ich schalt ihn wegen seines Betragens.

(u) zu + dative

†auffordern *invite to, call upon to*
beglückwünschen *congratulate on*
†berechtigen *entitle to*
†bestimmen *destine for*

†antreten *walk up to*
*anwachsen *increase to*
sich aufschwingen *rise to, bring o.s. to*

brauchen *need for*	†beitragen *contribute to*
†bringen (*irr.*) *provoke to, make*	†bewegen *induce, persuade to*
†dienen *serve to, for*	bitten *invite, ask s.b. to*
sich entwickeln *develop into*	einladen *invite to*
ernennen (*irr.*) *appoint*	†sich entschließen *decide to*
führen *lead to*	erziehen *educate, bring up to be s.th.*
gebrauchen *use for*	greifen *reach for*
gehören *belong, pertain to, be one*	†*kommen *come to*
of, be (integral) part of, be	†raten (D) *advise to (do s.th.)*
required for	*schmelzen *melt into*
*gelangen *get to*	sprechen *speak to*
gratulieren *congratulate on*	†treiben *drive to*
machen *make*	†verhelfen (D) *help to*
†neigen *incline, tend to*	*werden *become*
passen *go with, match*	†zwingen *force, compel to*
†provozieren *provoke to*	
steigern *intensify to*	
taugen *be fit for, be worth*	
†verdammen *condemn to*	
†verurteilen *sentence to*	
verweichen *soften into*	
wählen *elect*	
sich wenden (*irr.*) *turn to*	
sich umwenden (*irr.*) *turn round to*	

Die Krawatte paßt zu deinem Anzug. Das hat sicher zum Erfolg beigetragen. Dazu gehört Zeit. Wir brachten ihn zum Lachen (*made him laugh*). Wie sollte ich sie dazu bringen, mir alles zu erzählen?

(v) Clauses or infinitive phrases as prepositional object of (i) nouns and (ii) adjectives or past participles:

i   Das ist der Dank **dafür, daß** ich dich jahrelang gepflegt habe (*thanks for my having*).

Er machte keine ernsten Einwendungen **dagegen, daß** ich kommen sollte (*objections to my coming*).

Sie hatte große Angst **davor**, allein im Hause bleiben zu müssen (*fear of having to*).

Sie geben Ratschläge **darüber**, was für Befehle erteilt werden sollen (*advice as to what*).

ii Er war schuld **daran, daß** sie so elendiglich starb (*to blame for her having*).

Er war **damit** einverstanden, **daß** wir gehen sollten (*agreed that*).

Er war aufgebracht, ärgerlich, bestürzt, entrüstet, froh, traurig **darüber, daß** ich das gesagt hatte (*at my having said*).

Unabhängig **davon, daß** wir das wollten, beschloß auch er, hinzu-
gehen (*independently of the fact that*).
Ich bin weit **davon** entfernt, Ihre Meinung zu teilen (*far from sharing*).
Abgesehen **davon, daß** du zu jung bist, kennen wir den jungen Mann
noch nicht (*apart from the fact that*).
Was er sagt, ist nicht **danach** angetan, mir zu imponieren (*is not
calculated to impress me*).

80 The Infinitive-Noun

(a) Equivalent to the English gerund:

i Das Reisen ist jetzt sehr beliebt geworden. Das Schreiben muß
gelernt werden. Dies Abgeschnittensein (*being cut off*) von Nina ist
nicht zu ertragen (RINSER). Ich war des Wartens müde. Sie verfiel
dem Weinen (*lapsed into weeping*) (GRASS).

ii Vor dem Einschlafen (*before falling asleep*), während des langen
Wachens (*while remaining long awake*), nach dem Einschlafen (*after
falling asleep*).
Es geriet ins Wanken (*started wobbling*). Sie verlegten sich aufs Beten
(*turned to praying*). Er hinderte mich beim Essen (*prevented from eating*). Er munterte mich durch Kopfnicken auf (*encouraged by nodding*).
Die Unruhe äußerte sich im Zerreißen eines kleinen Zettels (*in the
action of tearing up*) (KAFKA). Beim Ein- und Aussteigen muß man
aufpassen (*when getting on and off*). Er war betäubt von dem plötz-
lichen Gewecktwerden aus tiefem Schlaf (*by being woken up*) (KAFKA).
Wir haben nur wenig Zeit zum Ausruhen (*for resting*). Sie wollte zum
Tanzen gehen (*go dancing*). Ist das kein Grund zum Lächeln (*for
smiling*)?

(b) Equivalent to the English infinitive:

Was gibt es zum Essen (*to eat*)? Er war bereit zum Weggehen (*to
go away*). Ich habe kein Geld zum Verschwenden (*to waste*). Er half
mir beim Suchen (*to look*). Das brachte ihn zum Lachen, Weinen,
Schreien, Reden, Schweigen (*made him laugh, cry, scream, talk, stop
talking*).

(c) Equivalent to the English 'enough to (make)' , (cf. 63(*d*)*iii*):

Es ist zum Rasendwerden (*enough to drive one mad*), voll zum Zer-
springen (*to bursting point*).

(d) Compound Infinitive-Nouns

Compound infinitive-nouns are not uncommon in German, ranging from
fairly simple ones like *das Vergessenwerden, das Sichgehenlassen, das Inein-
andergreifen* ('interlocking') to complicated ones like *das So-und-nicht-*

anders-sein (GUNDOLF) and *das Aufeinanderangewiesen- und abgestimmtsein der einzelnen Bauteile* ('the mutual interdependence and balancing of the separate parts of the structure') (W. SCHNEIDER).

Good examples of the use of compound infinitive-nouns are provided by the following passages:

> Auch fiel mir auf, daß Tätigkeiten wie Daumendrehen, Stirnrunzeln, Köpfchensenken, Händeschütteln, Falschgeldprägen, Lichtausknipsen, Zähneputzen, Totschießen und Trockenlegen überall ... geübt wurden (GRASS).

> Und endlich ... entsprang der Tanz ... Das war ein Wellenschlagen in den Sälen, ein Sich-Begegnen und ein Sich-Vermählen, ein Abschiednehmen und ein Wiederfinden, ein Glanzgenießen und ein Lichterblinden und ein Sich-Wiegen in den Sommerwinden, die in den Kleidern warmer Frauen sind (RILKE).

81 The Translation of the English Present Participle and Gerund

The following are common ways in which the English present participle and gerund may be translated. Compare also *63(a)(b)*, *64(a)(b)i*, *(c)(e)*, *79*, *80(a)(b)*.

(a) The infinitive with *zu* when there is no change of subject:

Es ist wunderschön, hier zu sein (*being*).

Ich gedenke/habe vor/beabsichtige/habe die Absicht, sie zu besuchen (*I intend visiting*).

Es gelang ihm, rechtzeitig zu Hause anzukommen (*succeeded in arriving*).

Ich hasse es/liebe es/ziehe es vor, zu Hause zu bleiben (*hate, love, prefer staying*).

Er saß da, ohne ein Wort zu sagen (*without saying*).

Er blieb sitzen, (an)statt aufzustehen (*instead of getting up*).

Menschen haben die Fähigkeit zu sprechen (*faculty of speaking*).

(b) A dependent clause introduced by *indem; dadurch, daß; ohne daß; (an)statt daß*:

Ich versuche abzunehmen, indem ich kein Brot esse (*by eating*).

Dadurch, daß du dich so benimmst, verdirbst du alles (*by behaving like that*). Man kann dadurch alles besser verstehen, daß man die Umstände in Betracht zieht (*by taking into account*).

Das Haus stand schon vor uns, ohne daß wir es erkannten (*without our recognising it*).

Anstatt daß er zu mir kommt, muß ich zu ihm gehen (*instead of his coming*).

(c) A dependent clause introduced by the causal conjunction *da* or by the temporal conjunctions *als, nachdem, bevor, ehe, wenn, wobei*:

Da er durstig war, trank er vier Tassen Tee (*being thirsty*).
Als er sich erholt hatte, ... (*having recovered*).
Nachdem er den Brief geschrieben hatte, ... (*after writing*).
Bevor ich einschlafe, ... (*before going to sleep*).
Indem er das sagte, lächelte er (*saying that, he smiled*).
Wenn man einen Brief schreibt, muß man mit dem Datum anfangen (*when/in writing a letter*).
Alle sahen zum Fenster hinaus, wobei sie unverständliche Gesten machten (*making*).

(d) A dependent simple infinitive after *hören* and *sehen*:

Ich hörte sie über die Brücke gehen (*heard them going*).
Sie sah ihn/ihren Mann sich entfernen (*saw him/her husband going away*).

(e) A dependent clause introduced by *wie* after *hören* and *sehen* and after other verbs of perception:

Er sah, wie sie über die Brücke ging (*saw her walking*).
Ich hörte, wie er die Treppe hinunterlief (*heard him running*).
Er sah zu/beobachtete, wie sie dort spielten (*watched them playing*).
Ich hörte ihr zu, wie sie Mozart spielte (*listened to her playing*).

(f) A relative clause:

Der Baum, der in der Ecke steht, ist ein Apfelbaum (*the tree standing*).
Ich bemerkte einen Mann, der neben meiner Frau saß (*sitting*).

(g) A main clause introduced by *und*:

Ich stand da und sah ihnen zu (*stood watching them*).

(h) An infinitive-noun construction introduced by *beim*:

Beim Einsteigen (*when/on/while getting in*) stolperte er.
Beim Erwachen (*on waking up*) bemerkte er sie.
Beim Überholen (*when overtaking*) muß man sehr aufpassen.

(i) The finite verb together with *gern, lieber, am liebsten*:

Ich bleibe gern zu Hause (*like staying*).
Ich tanze lieber (*prefer dancing*).
Ich gehe am liebsten ins Kino (*like best going*).

82 Exclamations

In exclamations the transposed order, with the verb coming at the end, is probably the most common; but both inverted order, with the subject following the verb, and interrogative order, where English asks a negative question, are frequently met with.

(a) Transposed order:

Wie die Zeit vergeht! Wie weit das ist! Wie viele Leute da sind! Wie nett das ist! Wie schön du das gemacht hast! Wie lange das her ist (*what a long time ago that is*)! Was für Geschichten sie erzählen konnte! Was für ein Mann das war! Was du nicht sagst (*you don't say so*)!

(b) Inverted order:

Wie ist das nett! Wie schön hast du das gemacht! Wie lange ist das her! Was für Geschichten konnte sie erzählen! Was haben wir gelacht (*how we laughed*)!

(c) Interrogative order:

Ist das schön (*isn't that lovely*)! Ach, bin ich froh (*aren't I glad*)!

(d) Without verbs:

Was für schlechtes Wetter! Was für eine schöne Überraschung! Welche große Auswahl! Welch ein guter Mann!

83 Some difficult German Words

(a) **auch**

Er kommt auch (*too, also, as well*). Sowohl er als auch ich (*both he and I*). Ich bin hungrig. – Ich auch (*so am I*). Ich habe es nicht gesehen. – Ich auch nicht (*nor have I*). Ohne auch nur mit der Wimper zu zucken (*without even batting an eyelid*). Wie dem auch sei (*however that may be*). So schön sie auch ist (*beautiful as she is*). Kann ich mich aber auch darauf verlassen (*can I really*)? Wenn auch (*so what!*)! Zum Donnerwetter auch (*confound it, no!*)!

(b) **denn**

Wo ist er denn (*then*)? Warum denn (*Why should I?*)? Warum denn nicht (*Why ever not?*)? Warum denn war ... (*So why was ...?*)? Was machen Sie denn da (*What on earth are you doing?*)? Er tut nichts, denn er ist faul (*for he is*). Er sorgte für mich mehr als Koch denn als Vater (*than as*). Ich werde nicht antworten, geschweige denn (*let alone*) Geld schicken.

(c) **doch**

Du bist doch nicht krank? – Doch (*You surely aren't ill, are you? – Yes I am*). Hilf mir doch (*Do help me*)! Sie hassen sich doch wirklich (*do really hate*). Du hast es doch gesagt (*after all, nevertheless*). Das müßtest du doch wissen ~~(You jolly well ought ...)~~. Wenn er doch käme (*if only*)! Er kommt doch (*He is coming, isn't he?*)? Er war müde, doch glücklich (*but*). Ungern erinnere ich mich dieser Sammlersonntage: unternahm ich doch an solch einem Tag ... (GRASS) (*for I undertook*).

(d) **etwa**

Etwa 20 Meilen weit (*about*). Könntest du es etwa morgen tun (*perhaps*)? Hat er es dir etwa angeboten (*by any chance*)? Haben Sie den Zug etwa auch verpaßt (*do you mean to say that ...*)? Sollte er Sie etwa danach fragen ... (*should he happen to*). Nicht etwa, daß ich etwas gegen ihn habe (*not that I really*). Er hat es nicht etwa mir zuliebe getan (*not exactly*).

(e) **immer**

Er kommt immer um diese Zeit (*always*). Lebe wohl auf immer (*for ever*)! Immer wenn er dabei war (*whenever*). Bleib so lange, wie immer du kannst (*as you possibly can*)! Er ist immer noch krank (*still*). Wo er auch immer ist (*wherever he*). Sie werden immer reicher (*richer and richer*). Immer wieder hat er das behauptet (*again and again*). Wann auch immer (*whenever*) du willst, ich komme.

(f) **irgend**

Wenn du irgend kannst (*possibly can*). Wenn es irgend möglich ist (*at all possible*). Irgendein/irgendwelches Buch (*any, some or other*); aus irgendeinem beliebigen Grund (*for any or every reason*); irgendeiner/irgend jemand (*somebody (or other*)); irgendwann (*some time or other*); irgendwie (*somehow or other, in a way, in any way*); irgendwo (*somewhere, anywhere*); irgendwo anders (*anywhere else*); irgend etwas/ irgendwas (*something or other, anything*).

(g) **ja**

Ja freilich (*why, to be sure*)! Sie ist ja ganz jung (*quite young, you know*). Du siehst ja ganz blaß aus (*you do look*). Du bist ja schon dagewesen (*Don't you remember, you ...*). Komm ja bald wieder (*be sure to*)! Ja so, ich ... (*Oh well, oh yes, I ...*). Die Idee ist alarmierend, ja schokkierend (*even*). Warum ißt du nicht? Ich esse ja (*But I am eating*).

(h) **mal**

Jetzt hör aber mal zu (*now just listen*)! Sie müssen mal kommen (*some day*). Hören Sie mal (*look here*)!

(i) **noch**

Er ist noch im Bett (*still*). Er ist noch nicht da (*not yet*). Er ist noch nie zu spät gekommen (*never before*). Er ist noch lange nicht gesund (*far from being*). Das ist noch billiger (*even cheaper*). Sie ist weder klug noch schön (*neither ... nor*). Nur noch ein Wort (*just one more*)! Ich habe ihn noch vor drei Tagen getroffen (*only 3 days ago*). Ich werde das noch heute tun (*this very day*).

(j) **nun** (**na** = colloquial form)

Nun, wie du willst (*Oh well ...*). Nun also (*now then, well then*). Nun ja, manchmal (*well*). Nun gut, ich bleibe (*all right*). Nun, los (*now, off you/we go!*)! Nun, nun (*steady! gently!*)! Nun (,da) er gekommen war, konnten wir ... (*now that*). Na, so was (*well, I never*)!

(k) **nur**

Nur noch eins (*just one other thing*). Warte nur (*Just you wait*)! Laß nur (*Please don't bother*)! Komm nur (*Come on*)! Nimm soviel du nur willst (*simply as much, whatever*)! Ich habe nur noch 2 Mark (*only 2 marks left*). Was sollen wir nur tun (*What on earth shall ...*)? Er tut nur so (*he's only pretending*). Wenn er nur käme (*if only*)!

(l) **recht**

An meiner rechten Seite (*right-hand*); auf der rechten Spur sein (*right*); es ist eine rechte Freude (*real*). Recht bald (*quite soon*); recht schönes Wetter (*quite nice*). Ich weiß nicht recht, ob ... (*quite*). Er tut mir recht leid (*truly sorry*). Wenn es dir recht ist ... (*if it suits you*). Das ist alles recht schön, aber ... (*all very well but ...*). Nun weint sie erst recht (*now ... all the more*). Du hast recht (*you are right*).

(m) **schon**

Ist die Post schon da (*already*)? Schon der Gedanke (*the very thought*). Schon an dem Nachmittag ... (*that very afternoon*). Das ist schon wahr, aber ... (*that is true enough, but*). Wir werden das schon schaffen (*we'll manage all right*). Er muß schon da sein (*by now*). Er hat schon genug Geld dafür ausgegeben (*enough as it is*). Schon gut (*all right, very well*)! Wenn schon (*so what!*)!

(n) **so**

Sie ist so schön (*so*). Sie ist genau/nicht so schön wie ihre Schwester (*just/not as*). So ungern ich es auch tat, ich mußte lächeln (*however unwillingly I*). Kommt er früh genug, so trifft er mich zu Hause (*then – or omit in translation*). So sind die Männer (*like that*). „Ich wollte nichts sagen." – „So?" (*Is that so? Really?*). So Gott will (*if it please God, God willing*). Der Ritter, so aus der Burg hervor/Vom Hange trabte in aller Früh (*the knight who*) (DROSTE-HÜLSHOFF).

(o) **wohl**

Mir ist (nicht) wohl ((*un-*)*well*). Leb wohl (*farewell*)! Wohl oder übel (*willy-nilly*). Sie sind wohl K. (*I suppose you ...*)? Es ist wohl an der

Zeit (*surely it*). Sie wird wohl keine Zeit haben (*I expect she*). Ob er wohl noch da ist (*I wonder whether* ...). Heute nicht, wohl aber morgen (*but perhaps*). Es hat wohl Zeit (*it is true*). Es ist wohl möglich, daß ... (*quite possible*). Er zeigte sich wohl ... (*he may be said to have shown himself*).

84 Synonyms

The following list deals exclusively with words occurring in the prose passages for translation and aims only at giving the fundamental distinctions.

TO ACCEPT: **annehmen** (general word); **akzeptieren** (find a person acceptable: *sie haben ihn nie akzeptiert*); **hinnehmen** (accept s.th. submissively); **sich abfinden mit** (accept a given situation, be reconciled to: *wir müssen uns damit abfinden*).

APPEARANCE: **das Aussehen** (external appearance of person); **das Äußere** (external appearance of person or thing); **der Schein** (appearance as opposed to reality: *der Schein trügt*, appearances are deceptive); **der Anschein** (outward show, semblance: *allem Anschein nach*, to all appearances); **das Erscheinen** (appearance of e.g. ghost, book, of person in court); **die Erscheinung** (1. appearance, presence: *sie ist eine stattliche Erscheinung*, a stately figure of a woman; 2. apparition, vision: *sie hatte Erscheinungen*; 3. phenomenon of nature); **die Gegenwart** (presence of somebody in a place).

ARM: **der Arm** (part of body); **die Armlehne** (of chair); **die Waffe** (weapon).

TO ASK: **fragen** (question: *er fragte mich, ob* ...; *er fragte mich nach dem Weg*); **stellen** (put: *er stellte mir eine Frage*); **bitten** (request: *er bat mich um Geld*; *er bat mich, um 2 Uhr da zu sein*); **einladen** (invite: *er lud mich zum Tee ein*); **verlangen/fordern** (demand: *das ist zu viel verlangt/gefordert*); **auffordern** (call upon to do s.th., request, summon: *eine Dame zum Tanz auffordern*; *man forderte ihn auf, den Saal zu verlassen*).

TO BE: **sein** (be: *er ist jung; es sind viele da*); **es gibt** (there is/are: *es gibt Leute, die; was gibt's zum Essen?*); **sich befinden** (find o.s., be situated: *das Haus befindet sich an der Ecke*); **liegen** (lie: *das Buch liegt auf dem Tisch*); **stehen** (stand; *der Weg steht offen; der Fluß stand hoch*); **entstehen** (arise, occur: *es entstand eine Pause*); **sich verhalten** (be the case: *die Sache verhält sich anders*).

N.B. German prefers a more specific word to render 'to be' wherever possible.

TO BEHAVE: **sich benehmen** (refers to the good or bad manners of individuals: *er benahm sich gut/schlecht*); **sich betragen** (refers to conduct, the observance of codes of behaviour: *er hat sich unfreundlich* *gegen uns betragen*); **sich verhalten** (refers to the way things react, or to the psychological attitude of individuals or peoples: *man muß sich in solchen Umständen vorsichtig verhalten*).

BEHAVIOUR, CONDUCT, MANNERS: **das Benehmen** (manners, good or bad); **das Betragen** (conduct, e.g. in school); **das Verhalten** (reaction of things, attitude of individuals and peoples).

TO BELONG: **gehören** (D) (be rightful possession of: *das Buch gehört mir*); **gehören zu** (be part of, be connected with: *alles, was zum Leben gehört*; *er gehört zur Familie*); **angehören** (to be a property or attribute of; be a member of a community: *das gehört dem Geist an; er gehört dem deutschen Staat an*)..

BOX, CASE: **der Kasten** (solid, well-made, cf. *der Briefkasten*); **die Kiste** (wooden chest for despatching goods, cf. *die Teekiste*); **der Koffer** (suit-case); **der Reisekoffer** (travelling-trunk); **die Truhe** (article of furniture, e.g. rug-chest); **die Schachtel** (flimsy box, often of cardboard, cf. *die Hutschachtel, eine Schachtel Streichhölzer*, a box of matches); **das Kästchen** (casket, e.g. for jewels); **das Etui** (case, e.g. for cigarettes); **der Fall** (instance: *in dem Fall kann ich nicht kommen*).

TO CATCH: **fangen** (general word: *er fing den Ball, den Vogel, den Verbrecher*); **auffangen** (catch s.th. rapidly moving, intercept, e.g. light, glance, words); **erreichen** (reach in time: *sie erreichte gerade noch den Zug*); **nehmen** (take, e.g. a train regularly: *sie nimmt jeden Tag den 8-Uhr-Zug*); **erhaschen** (just manage to catch: *er konnte nur einen Blick von ihr erhaschen*); **gefangennehmen** (capture, take prisoner); **erblicken** (catch sight of); **flüchtig sehen** (catch a glimpse of); **sich erkälten** (catch cold); **sich verfangen** (get caught in: *ihre Hand verfing sich in dem Stoff ihres Kleides*).

TO COMMAND: *see* TO ORDER

TO GET: **werden** (become); **haben** (have); **bekommen** (acquire); **geraten in** (A) (get into, e.g. difficulties); **geraten unter** (A) (get among); **geraten zu** (get to a place); **einsteigen in** (A) (get into, e.g. train); **aufstehen** (get up); **heruntergehen** (get off, e.g. table); **hinübergehen** (get across); **gelangen zu** (come to); **zurückkommen** (get back); **nach Hause kommen** (get home); **kommen zu** (get away to); **auskommen** (get along, manage); **gut auskommen mit** (get on with s.b.).

INTERVAL: **der Abstand** (distance away from: *in regelmäßigen Abständen*); **die Pause** (period between lessons, acts of play, etc.); **die Zwischenzeit** (intervening period).

JEWEL(RY), GEM: **der Schmuck** (jewelry – general word); **das Juwel** (very precious jewel: *die Kronjuwelen*); **der Edelstein** (precious stone); **das Kleinod (-ien)** (gem).

TO KNOW: **kennen** (know persons or things); **kennenlernen** (get to know); **wissen** (know facts through having learnt them: *ich weiß, daß ich nichts weiß; er weiß das Gedicht auswendig; er weiß zu schweigen*, knows how to hold his tongue); **Bescheid wissen** (be well informed: *er weiß gut Bescheid in seinem Fach*, he knows his subject); **können** (know a language: *er kann (kein) Deutsch*); **bekannt sein** (be (well-) known).

KNOWLEDGE: **die Kenntnis** (a good acquaintance with s.th.: *seine Kenntnis der Kunst; seine Kenntnisse in der Mathematik*); **das Wissen** (knowledge that s.th. is the case, also general organised knowledge: *ohne mein Wissen; er hat ein gründliches Wissen*); **die Wissenschaft** (scholarship, learning).

TO LEAVE: **lassen** (leave s.th. or s.o. somewhere or in a certain state: *sie ließen ihn dort liegen*); **verlassen** (1. leave a place: *er hat das Haus, die Schule, Paris verlassen*; 2. leave a person behind, abandon s.o.: *er hat seine Frau verlassen*); **im Stich lassen** (leave in the lurch, abandon: *er mußte seine Arbeit im Stich lassen*); **überlassen** (leave s.th. to s.b. else: *überlassen Sie es mir!*); **hinterlassen** (bequeath: *er hat ihr sein ganzes Vermögen hinterlassen*).

TO LOOK: **aussehen** (look like, have the look of: *Sie sehen ganz wie ein Professor aus*); **(von oben bis unten) mustern** (look s.b. up and down); **ansehen** (look at for some space of time: *er sah uns freundlich an*); **sehen auf** (A) (glance at: *er sah auf die Uhr*); **sich (D) ansehen** (have a good look at: *er sah sich (D) die Stadt an*); **aufblicken/emporblicken/aufsehen/emporsehen** (look up: *er blickte/sah zu ihr auf*); **herabblicken** (look down); **suchen (nach)** (look for: *er hat es überall gesucht; er suchte nach einer Ausrede*); **auf der Suche sein nach** (look for, be on the look-out for: *wir waren auf der Suche nach einer Furt* (ford)); **pflegen** (look after, tend: *sie pflegte den Kranken*).

MATTER: **die Materie/der Stoff** (philosophical term, 'matter' as opposed to 'mind': *die Philosophie stellt Geist und Materie/Stoff einander gegenüber*); **der Stoff** (material for s.th.: *Stoff zum Lesen*, reading matter); **die Sache** (unimportant matter or affair; *das ist Ansichtssache*, matter of opinion; also=(good) cause: *die gute Sache*); **die Angelegenheit** (a matter of some weight: *wichtige Angelegenheiten*); **das Ding** (thing: *wie die Dinge liegen*, as matters stand; *naturwissenschaftliche Dinge*); **der Gegenstand** (subject-matter).
Note also: **tatsächlich** (as a matter of fact); **nüchtern** (matter-of-fact: *ein nüchterner Mensch*); **es handelt sich um** (A)/**es ist eine Frage** + (G) (it is a matter of); **was hast du?** (what is the matter with you?); **das ist etwas anderes** (that is another matter).

MAN, MEN, PEOPLE, PERSON, PERSONAGE: **man** (one, people in general: *man sagt, daß* ...); **jemand** (a man, somebody); **einer, der...** (a man who ...); **derjenige, der** ... (the man who ...); **Leute** (people:

eine Menge Leute; es gibt Leute, die …); **die** (-**jenigen**), **die** … (people who, the persons who); **der Mensch** (human being: *andere Menschen,* other persons; *so sind die Menschen,* people are like that; *der Mensch ist frei geschaffen,* man is created free); **der Mann** (man, as opposed to woman); **das Volk** (people = nation; *das englische Volk; die Völker der Welt*); **die Person** (1. person, individual: *jede Person zahlt eine Mark; ein Tisch für zwei Personen; die Familie besteht aus sechs Personen*; 2. personage: *königliche Personen,* royal personages; 3. character in a play: *die handelnden Personen,* dramatis personae; *die Hauptpersonen,* leading characters; *die Nebenpersonen,* minor characters).

TO NEED: **brauchen** (need to, want s.th. or s.b.: *Sie brauchen nicht zu kommen; ich brauche Ruhe*); **benötigen** (require, need for some purpose: *er benötigt Zeit, meine Hilfe*); **erfordern** (of things, demand: *die Situation erfordert Takt, Vorstellungskraft*); **bedürfen** (be in need of: *wir bedürfen der Ruhe; es bedarf nur eines Wortes,* only one word is needed); **genügen** (need but: *ein Blick genügte, um …*, it needed but one glance); **notwendig sein** (be needed: *nur eines ist notwendig,* only one thing is needed).

NEED: **die Not** (distress, need: *in Not/Nöten sein*); **die Notwendigkeit** (necessity to do s.th.: *eine Notwendigkeit erkennen*); **der Bedarf** (requirements: *Bedarf an Menschen und Materialien*); **es ist nicht notwendig, zu** … (there is no need to …); **das Bedürfnis** (need of/for).

TO ORDER, COMMAND: **befehlen** (to command: *er befahl mir zu schweigen*); **gebieten** (enjoin, command – a more lofty term); **heißen** (bid, a command given orally: *er hieß mich hereinkommen*); **bestellen** (order goods: *wir bestellten zwei Glas Bier*).

ORDER, COMMAND, COMMANDMENT: **der Befehl** (order, command: *Befehle erteilen/geben; Befehle ausführen*); **das Gebot** (commandment: *die zehn Gebote*); **die Bestellung** (order for goods: *eine Bestellung auf/für 10 Pfund Zucker*); **das Kommando** (command, authority: *das seinem Kommando zu übergebende Schiff*); **die Beherrschung** (command of a subject or emotion: *seine Beherrschung der Gemütsregungen*).

PLAY: **das Spiel** (game; also play, e.g. of light); **der Spielraum** (play = scope: *wir haben nicht genug Spielraum gehabt*); **der Scherz** (jest: *im Scherz,* in play).

TO PUT: **legen** (put in lying position); **stellen** (put in upright or standing position); **setzen** (put in sitting position: *setz das Kind auf den Stuhl*); **stecken** (put, e.g. into a pocket); **drücken** (put, e.g. into s.o.'s hand: *er drückte ihm ein Geldstück in die Hand*); **anziehen** (put on clothes); **aufsetzen** (put on hat, spectacles); **umschnallen** (put on belt); **ins Bett bringen** (put into bed); **entrücken** (D) (put beyond, e.g. reach: *der Tod hat ihn allen Sorgen entrückt*).

RATHER: **ziemlich** (fairly: *ziemlich spät, weit*); **recht** (quite: *sie ist recht hübsch*); **etwas** (somewhat: *eine etwas melodische Stimme*);

(84)

irgendwie (somehow or other: *irgendwie rührend*); lieber (preferably: *ich komme lieber später*); mehr (more: *mehr aus Furcht als aus Liebe*); eher (more correctly: *eher ehrenswert als intelligent*).

TO REALISE: begreifen (grasp, understand: *ich fange an zu begreifen, warum ...*); sich bewußt sein (be aware of: *ich bin mir der Wichtigkeit des Problems bewußt*); einem klar werden (become clear to one: *es wurde mir endlich klar, daß ...*); sich vergegenwärtigen (*bring vividly before one's mind: man muß sich vergegenwärtigen, was die Folgen sein werden*).

REALLY: eigentlich (strictly speaking, as a matter of fact; *eigentlich hätte ich nicht kommen sollen*); wirklich (undoubtedly: *es ist wirklich wahr*); endlich einmal (positively, indeed: *der Regen muß endlich einmal aufhören*).

TO SEE: sehen (general word); erblicken (catch sight of); ansehen (look at); sich (D) ansehen (see for oneself: *sehen Sie es sich mal an*); halten für (see as, consider as: *sie hielten ihn für unfreundlich*); sorgen für (see to s.th.: *er sorgt dafür, daß sie alles hat*); einsehen (understand: *er hat eingesehen, daß ich das nicht machen kann*); ach so (*oh I see*); ja, ich verstehe schon (*yes, I see*); siehst du? (*you see*).

SO: so (so: *ich bin so müde*); deshalb (therefore, and so: *deshalb habe ich angerufen*); auch (also: *Er ist müde. – Ich auch*, so am I); es (it: *ich sagte es dir*, I told you so).

TO TAKE: nehmen (general word); mitnehmen (take with one); ergreifen (seize, take up, e.g. arms); sich beteiligen an (D) (take part in); irreführen/hinters Licht führen (take in, deceive); entnehmen (D) (take from: *er hat es diesem Buch entnommen*); annehmen (take on, assume, e.g. an appearance); abnehmen (take off, e.g. hat); ausziehen (take off, e.g. clothes); zurücktreten (take (a step) back); antreten (enter upon: *ein Amt antreten*); vertreten (adopt: *einen Standpunkt vertreten*, take a stand); halten für (take for: *ich hielt ihn für ein Genie*); ansehen als (take as: *ich sehe es als Kompliment an*); brauchen (need: *er brauchte lange Zeit, um es zu tun*). Note also: Maßnahmen treffen (take steps); stattfinden (take place).

TO THINK: denken (general word); denken an (A) (think of: *woran denken Sie?*); denken/halten von (have opinion of; *was denken/halten Sie von ihm?*); nachdenken über (A) (reflect, think over: *wir müssen zuerst darüber nachdenken*); glauben (believe: *ich glaube nicht, daß er kommt*); sich vorstellen (imagine, conceive: *ich kann mir nicht vorstellen, was sie damit meint*); meinen (be of the opinion).

THOUGHT: der Gedanke (idea); das Denken (thinking)

VERY: sehr (very: *es ist sehr spät*); schon (already: *schon an dem Nachmittag*, that very afternoon; *schon ihre Grenzen*, its very boundaries); genau (exactly: *genau in der Mitte*, in the very middle); aller- (of all:

105

das allergrößte Glück, the very greatest good fortune); **äußerst**
(extreme: *am äußersten Rande,* at the very edge).

WELL: **wohl** (well: *ihm ist wohl; leben Sie wohl!; du weißt wohl, daß ...*,
you know quite well that ...); **gut** (well: *schlafen Sie gut!; so gut man
kann*); **gesund** (healthy: *er ist gesund*); **sowohl** (as well: *er sowohl wie/
als ich; sowohl er als ich,* he as well as I); **ebensogut** (just as well:
du kannst ebensogut morgen kommen) ; **nun** (well: *nun, was meinen Sie?*
well, what do you think?); **nun gut** (well, all right); **ja schon** (well yes,
i.e. with some reservations; *Magst du ihn? – Ja schon*); **ja** (well, perhaps, i.e. embarrassed or impatient: *Willst du das haben? – Ja, ich weiß
nicht*).

85 Punctuation, Hyphenation and the Character ß

Indications as to punctuation are only given when German usage differs
from English.

(a) The comma (*das Komma/der Beistrich*) is used in German:

i Before *aber, sondern, und zwar, und das* and *und* preceding another
conjunction:

Du bist schön, aber hart. Nicht nur du, sondern auch er. Ich werde
schreiben, und zwar bald. Er lehnte ab, und das mit Würde. Er war
viel zu lange dort geblieben, und weil er es jetzt eilig hatte, mußte er
sehr schnell fahren.

ii Between main clauses, even when these are linked by *und* or *oder*,
except when the clauses are very short or where the (same) subject
is not repeated:

Er stand auf, er ging zur Tür, und er öffnete sie.
Ihr müßt arbeiten, oder ihr fallt durch.

But Er setzte sich und er las. Er pfiff oder er sang. Er ging zur Tür und
öffnete sie.

iii Between a subordinate clause and a main clause:

Da es spät war, mußte er sich beeilen.
Er wußte, daß es spät war.

iv Before the simple infinitive with *zu* when it is the complement of the
subject of the clause, when *zu* is the equivalent of *um zu*, or when the
infinitive is itself followed by another infinitive with *zu*:

Seine Hoffnung war, durchzukommen. Er kommt, zu helfen.
Er wurde nicht müde, zu lesen und zu lernen.

But Er war immer bereit zu helfen. Er wünschte zu kommen.
Es begann zu regnen. Es hat zu regnen begonnen. Er befahl ihm zu
gehen.

v To separate an extended participle or infinitive (but not a simple participle or infinitive) from the clause:

An der Tür lehnend, rauchte er seine Zigarre. Er arbeitete zwei Stunden lang, ohne aufzuhören. Er arbeitete schwer, um durchzukommen. Er versuchte, ins Haus zu kommen.
But Schweigend arbeitete er weiter. Er versuchte zu antworten.

vi Before the extended infinitive after the verbs *haben, hoffen, pflegen* and *glauben* when these verbs are in some way qualified, but not otherwise:

Er hoffte sehr/doch, sie am nächsten Morgen zu sehen.
Er pflegte damals, sie zu besuchen. Ich glaube bestimmt, das gehört zu haben.
But Er hatte nichts zu sagen. Er hoffte sie zu Hause zu finden. Er pflegte sie jeden Tag zu besuchen. Er glaubte kommen zu können.

vii After an infinitive (simple with *zu* or extended) when this comes first in the sentence immediately followed by a demonstrative (*das, daran, darauf,* etc.), but not otherwise:

Früh aufzustehen, das ist höchst unangenehm. Zu arbeiten, daran hatten wir wirklich nicht gedacht.
But Früh aufzustehen ist höchst unangenehm.

(b) Inverted commas (*Anführungszeichen*) are used as in English but are written and printed differently:

„Er kommt bald", sagte er. „Bleib da!"

(c) The colon (*der Doppelpunkt*) is used in German to introduce direct speech:

Er sagte zu mir: „Ich muß jetzt unbedingt nach Hause gehen."

(d) The exclamation mark (*das Ausrufezeichen*) is used after imperatives, optative clauses, exclamations and after the salutation in a letter:

Bleib sitzen! Wenn er doch käme! Auf Wiedersehen!
Schade! Wie blaß du aussiehst!
Liebe Trude! – Ich danke Dir ... Sehr geehrter Herr! (*Dear Sir*).

(e) The full-stop (*der Punkt*), semi-colon (*der Strichpunkt/das Semikolon*), question-mark (*das Fragezeichen*), dash (*der Gedankenstrich*), brackets (*Klammern*) and points of suspension (*Auslassungspunkte*) are used as in English.

(f) Hyphenation:

i The syllable after the hyphen should if possible begin with a consonant:

lie-gen; nä-hern; Bru-der

ii   *ch*, *sch*, *ß*, *ph*, *th* are never separated:

    Lö-cher; Fi-scher; Fü-ße; pro-phezeien; ka-tholisch

iii Of several consonants with other combinations the last follows the hyphen:

    sin-gen; Fül-le; Wech-sel; Abwechs-lung

NOTE 1: *ck* becomes *k-k*: lok-ken; Bäk-ker
NOTE 2: *st* is never separated except in compound words: La-ster; Fa-sten; *but* Diens-tag

iv Suffixes beginning with a vowel take with them the preceding consonant:

    Lehre-rin; Freun-din; Hoff-nung; Bäcke-rei

v A single vowel should not be separated from the rest of the word:

    aber; *not* a-ber

vi A word may be hyphenated between two vowels only when there is a clear break between them:

    be-enden; Genugtu-ung; Befrei-ung; Mau-er
But Waa-ge; Boo-te; Bei-ne; Häu-ser; Beu-tel

vii In compound words the division comes at the end of each constituent element:

    Last-auto; dar-aus; wor-auf; Geburts-tags-geschenk

viii Hyphenation of the constituent elements themselves follows the same rules as those given above (i)–(vi):

    Ge-burts-tags-ge-schenk; Auf-fas-sungs-ver-mö-gen

(g) The character *ß*

In printing, the character *ß* is used for *ss*:

i medially, when preceded by a long vowel or by a diphthong:

    Mäße; Größe; Muße; Füße; regelmäßig; fleißig; äußerst; draußen
But Mässe; Bissen; Flüsse; essen; lässig; Hausschlüssel

ii at the end of a word or syllable with or without *t* following, whether the vowel preceding is long or short:

    däß; Mäß; gewiß; Gewißheit; Mißachtung; Mißfallen; Kompromiß; laß; mußt; mußte
But gewisse; Kompromisse; lasse

NOTE: If, after a short vowel, the omission of a final *e* is indicated by an apostrophe, *ss* is used, not *ß*, e.g. *lass'*.

iii when followed by a consonant as a result of elision of unstressed *e*:

    laßt; ein Gottverlaßner
But lasset; ein Gottverlassener

In writing it is not necessary to use the character *ß*. If, however, it is used the rules given above should be observed.

86 Strong and Weak Declension

(a) Strong Declension					(b) Weak Declension			
	sing.		*pl.*			*sing.*		*pl.*	
	m.	*f.*	*n.*	*m.f.n.*		*m.*	*f.*	*n.*	*m.f.n.*
N.	– er	– e	– es	– e		– c	– e	– e	– en
A.	– en	– e	– es	– e		– en	– e	– e	– en
G.	– es	– er	– es	– er		– en	– en	– en	– en
D.	– em	– er	– em	– en		– en	– en	– en	– en

NOTE 1: Though the terms 'strong' and 'weak' are also applied by grammarians to the declension of nouns (see *101*), the above inflections do not apply to nouns.

NOTE 2: The attributive adjective declined strong has in modern German the weak form *-en* and not the strong form *-es* in the genitive singular masculine and neuter (see *93*).

NOTE 3: A few other words, e.g. *jeder, aller*, when declined strong, are now often found with the weak ending *-en* in the genitive singular masculine and neuter in front of nouns that clearly show the genitive case. Thus:

> Die Lösung jedes/jeden Problems.
> Trotz alles/allen Widerstands.
> *But* Die Aufgabe jedes einzelnen.
> Die Entbehrung alles Gewohnten.

87 Declension of the Definite Article

	sing.			*pl.*
	m.	*f.*	*n.*	*m.f.n.*
N.	der	die	das·	die
A.	den	die	das	die
G.	des	der	des	der
D.	dem	der	dem	den

88 Declension of the Indefinite Article

	m.	*f.*	*n.*
N.	ein	eine	ein
A.	einen	eine	ein
G.	eines	einer	eines
D.	einem	einer	einem

NOTE: As with English 'a' there is no plural of *ein*. The plural of *ein Mann* is simply *Männer*.

89 Declension of the Possessive Adjective

	sing.			pl.
	m.	*f.*	*n.*	*m.f.n.*
N.	mein	meine	mein	meine
A.	meinen	meine	mein	meine
G.	meines	meiner	meines	meiner
D.	meinem	meiner	meinem	meinen

Likewise: *dein, sein, ihr, unser, euer, Ihr* and *kein.*

90 Declension of the Demonstrative Adjective and Pronoun

	sing.			pl.
	m.	*f.*	*n.*	*m.f.n.*
N.	dieser	diese	dieses	diese
A.	diesen	diese	dieses	diese
G.	dieses	dieser	dieses	dieser
D.	diesem	dieser	diesem	diesen

Likewise: *jener, welcher, solcher, mancher, jeder* (sing.), *alle* (pl.), *einige* (pl.), *etliche* (pl.), *mehrere* (pl.), *viele* (pl.), *wenige* (pl.). (See also *51*.)

91 Inflection of the Adjective after the Definite Article

	sing.			pl.
	m.	*f.*	*n.*	*m.f.n.*
N.	der – e	die – e	das – e	die – en
A.	den – en	die – e	das – e	die – en
G.	des – en	der – en	des – en	der – en
D.	dem – en	der – en	dem – en	den – en

Likewise after: *dieser, jener, welcher, solcher, derselbe, derjenige, jeder* (sing.), *alle* (pl.), *mancher* (sing.)

92 Inflection of the Adjective after the Possessive Adjective

	sing.			pl.
	m.	*f.*	*n.*	*m.f.n.*
N.	mein – er	meine – e	mein – es	meine – en
A.	meinen – en	meine – e	mein – es	meine – en
G.	meines – en	meiner – en	meines – en	meiner – en
D.	meinem – en	meiner – en	meinem – en	meinen – en

Likewise after: *dein, sein, ihr, unser, euer, Ihr, ein* (sing.) and *kein.*

93 Inflection of the Adjective when standing alone before a Noun

	sing.			*pl.*
	m.	*f.*	*n.*	*m.f.n.*
N.	- er	- e	- es	- e
A.	- en	- e	- es	- e
G.	- en	- er	- en	- er
D.	- em	- er	- em	- en

Likewise after the plurals: *2, 3, 4,* etc. (but no genitive except with 2 and 3) *ein paar, einige, etliche, manche, mehrere, viele* and *wenige.*

94 Declension of *derselbe* and *derjenige*

	sing.			*pl.*
	m.	*f.*	*n.*	*m.f.n.*
N.	derselbe	dieselbe	dasselbe	dieselben
A.	denselben	dieselbe	dasselbe	dieselben
G.	desselben	derselben	desselben	derselben
D.	demselben	derselben	demselben	denselben

Likewise: *derjenige.*

95 Declension of the Relative Pronoun

		sing.			*pl.*
		m.	*f.*	*n.*	*m.f.n.*
(a)	*N.*	der	die	das	die
	A.	den	die	das	die
	G.	**dessen**	**deren**	**dessen**	**deren**
	D.	dem	der	dem	**denen**
(b)	*N.*	welcher	welche	welches	welche
	A.	welchen	welche	welches	welche
	G.	(dessen)	(deren)	(dessen)	(deren)
	D.	welchem	welcher	welchem	welchen

96 Declension of *wer, was*

	m.f.	*n.*
N.	wer	was
A.	wen	was (wodurch, worein, etc.)
G.	wessen	wessen
D.	wem	(womit, worauf, etc.)

97 Declension of the Demonstrative Pronoun

	sing.			*pl.*
	m.	*f.*	*n.*	*m.f.n.*
N.	der	die	das	die
A.	den	die	das	die
G.	**dessen**	**deren**	**dessen**	**deren/derer**
D.	dem	der	dem	**denen**

NOTE: The genitive plural of the demonstrative pronoun is **derer** when followed by a relative pronoun.

98 Declension of the Personal Pronouns

sing.	N.	ich	du	Sie	er	sie	es
	A.	mich	dich	Sie	ihn	sie	es
	G.	meiner	deiner	Ihrer	seiner	ihrer	seiner
	D.	mir	dir	Ihnen	ihm	ihr	ihm
pl.	N.	wir	ihr	Sie		sie	
	A.	uns	euch	Sie		sie	
	G.	unser	euer	Ihrer		ihrer	
	D.	uns	euch	Ihnen		ihnen	

99 Declension of the Reflexive Pronouns

sing.	A.	mich	dich	sich	sich
	G.	meiner	deiner	Ihrer selbst	seiner/ihrer selbst
	D.	mir	dir	sich	sich
pl.	A.	uns	euch	sich	sich
	G.	unser	euer	Ihrer selbst	ihrer selbst
	D.	uns	euch	sich	sich

100 Declension of the Possessive Pronouns

		sing.			*pl.*
		m.	*f.*	*n.*	*m.f.n.*
(a) N.		mein**er**	mein**e**	mein(**e**)**s**	mein**e**
A.		mein**en**	mein**e**	mein(**e**)**s**	mein**e**
G.		mein**es**	mein**er**	mein**es**	mein**er**
D.		mein**em**	mein**er**	mein**em**	mein**en**
(b) N.	der mein**e**	die mein**e**	das mein**e**	die mein**en**
A.	den mein**en**	die mein**e**	das mein**e**	die mein**en**
G.	des mein**en**	der mein**en**	des mein**en**	der mein**en**
D.	dem mein**en**	der mein**en**	dem mein**en**	den mein**en**
(c) N.	der mein**ige**	die mein**ige**	das mein**ige**	die mein**igen**
A.	den mein**igen**	die mein**ige**	das mein**ige**	die mein**igen**
G.	des mein**igen**	der mein**igen**	des mein**igen**	der mein**igen**
D.	dem mein**igen**	der mein**igen**	dem mein**igen**	den mein**igen**

Likewise: *deiner, seiner, ihrer, unserer, eurer, Ihrer.* Like (a): *einer, keiner.*

101 Declension of Nouns

	STRONG						WEAK	MIXED	
	Ia		Ib		Ic		II	IIIa	IIIb
	Pl. not modified	Pl. modified	Pl. not modified	Pl. modified	Pl. not modified	Pl. modified			
Masc.									
Sing. N.	Tag	Sohn	(3) Geist	(10) Wald	Onkel	Apfel	Mensch	Staat	(10) Name
A.	Tag	Sohn	Geist	Wald	Onkel	Apfel	Menschen	Staat	Namen
G.	Tag(e)s	Sohn(e)s	Geistes	Wald(e)s	Onkels	Apfels	Menschen	Staat(e)s	Namens
D.	Tag(e)	Sohn(e)	Geist(e)	Wald(e)	Onkel	Apfel	Menschen	Staat(e)	Namen
Pl. N.	Tage	Söhne	Geister	Wälder	Onkel	Äpfel	Menschen	Staaten	Namen
A.	Tage	Söhne	Geister	Wälder	Onkel	Äpfel	Menschen	Staaten	Namen
G.	Tage	Söhne	Geister	Wälder	Onkel	Äpfel	Menschen	Staaten	Namen
D.	Tagen	Söhnen	Geistern	Wäldern	Onkeln	Äpfeln	Menschen	Staaten	Namen
Fem.									
Sing. N.	(10) Trübsal	(30) Stadt	None	None	None	(2) Mutter	None	Frau	None
A.	Trübsal	Stadt				Mutter		Frau	
G.	Trübsal	Stadt				Mutter		Frau	
D.	Trübsal	Stadt				Mutter		Frau	
Pl. N.	Trübsale	Städte				Mütter		Frauen	
A.	Trübsale	Städte				Mütter		Frauen	
G.	Trübsale	Städte				Mütter		Frauen	
D.	Trübsalen	Städten				Müttern		Frauen	
Neut.									
Sing. N.	Tier	(1) Floß	Kind	Haus	Fenster	(1) Kloster	None	(7) Bett	(1) Herz
A.	Tier	Floß	Kind	Haus	Fenster	Kloster		Bett	Herz
G.	Tier(e)s	Floßes	Kind(e)s	Hauses	Fensters	Klosters		Bett(e)s	Herzens
D.	Tier(e)	Floß(e)	Kind(e)	Haus(e)	Fenster	Kloster		Bett(e)	Herzen
Pl. N.	Tiere	Flöße	Kinder	Häuser	Fenster	Klöster		Betten	Herzen
A.	Tiere	Flöße	Kinder	Häuser	Fenster	Klöster		Betten	Herzen
G.	Tiere	Flöße	Kinder	Häuser	Fenster	Klöster		Betten	Herzen
D.	Tieren	Flößen	Kindern	Häusern	Fenstern	Klöstern		Betten	Herzen

NOTE: The approximate number of nouns, excluding compound nouns, in the various groups is given where this is not large.

102 Alphabetical list of Strong and Irregular Verbs

Infinitive	3rd Pers. Sing. Pres.	3rd Pers. Sing. Impf.	Past Part.	Meaning
backen	bäckt[1]	buk[1]	gebacken	bake
befehlen	befiehlt	befahl[2]	befohlen	order
beginnen	beginnt	begann	begonnen	begin
beißen	beißt	biß	gebissen	bite
bergen	birgt	barg	geborgen	shelter; contain
*bersten	birst	barst	geborsten	burst (intr.)
betrügen	betrügt	betrog	betrogen	deceive, cheat
bewegen	bewegt	bewog	bewogen	induce
(*)biegen	biegt	bog	gebogen	bend, turn
bieten	bietet	bot	geboten	offer, bid
binden	bindet	band	gebunden	tie
bitten	bittet	bat	gebeten	ask, request
blasen	bläst	blies	geblasen	blow, sound
*bleiben	bleibt	blieb	geblieben	remain, stay
braten	brät	briet	gebraten	roast
(*)brechen	bricht	brach	gebrochen	break
brennen	brennt	brannte[3]	gebrannt	burn
bringen	bringt	brachte[3]	gebracht	bring, take
denken	denkt	dachte[3]	gedacht	think
(*)dringen	dringt	drang	gedrungen	press; insist
dürfen[4]	darf	durfte	gedurft	be allowed to
empfehlen	empfiehlt	empfahl[2]	empfohlen	recommend
*erlöschen[5]	erlischt	erlosch	erloschen	be extinguished
*erschrecken[6]	erschrickt	erschrak	erschrocken	be frightened
erwägen	erwägt	erwog	erwogen	think over, weigh
essen	ißt	aß	gegessen	eat
(*)fahren	fährt	fuhr	gefahren	go (not on foot); drive
*fallen	fällt	fiel	gefallen	fall
fangen	fängt	fing	gefangen	catch
fechten	ficht[7]	focht	gefochten	fight, fence
finden	findet	fand	gefunden	find
flechten	flicht[8]	flocht	geflochten	wreathe
(*)fliegen	fliegt	flog	geflogen	fly
(*)fliehen	flieht	floh	geflohen	flee
*fließen	fließt	floß	geflossen	flow
fressen	frißt	fraß	gefressen	eat (of animals)
(*)frieren	friert	fror	gefroren	freeze, be cold

[1] Also: backt, backte
[2] See 70 (e)
[3] See 70 (f)
[4] See 67

[5] Weak = extinguish
[6] Weak = frighten
[7] 2nd person singular du fichtst
[8] 2nd person singular du flichtst

Infinitive	3rd Pers. Sing. Pres.	3rd Pers. Sing. Impf.	Past Part.	Meaning
gebären	gebiert	gebar	geboren	give birth, bear
geben	gibt	gab	gegeben	give
*gedeihen	gedeiht	gedieh	gediehen	prosper, flourish
*gehen	geht	ging	gegangen	go, walk
*gelingen[1]	gelingt	gelang	gelungen	succeed
gelten	gilt	galt	gegolten	be valid, worth
*genesen	genest	genas	genesen	grow well, recover
genießen	genießt	genoß	genossen	enjoy
*geschehen	geschieht	geschah	geschehen	happen
gewinnen	gewinnt	gewann	gewonnen	win, gain
gießen	gießt	goß	gegossen	pour
gleichen	gleicht	glich	geglichen	resemble
*gleiten	gleitet	glitt	geglitten	glide, slide
glimmen	glimmt	glomm	geglommen	glow
graben	gräbt	grub	gegraben	dig
greifen	greift	griff	gegriffen	grasp, seize grab
haben[2]	hat	hatte	gehabt	have
halten	hält	hielt	gehalten	hold, stop (intr.)
hängen[3]	hängt	hing	gehangen	hang (intr.)
hauen	haut	hieb[4]	gehauen	hew; beat; chop
heben	hebt	hob	gehoben	raise, lift
heißen	heißt	hieß	geheißen	be called; bid
helfen	hilft	half[5]	geholfen	help
kennen	kennt	kannte[6]	gekannt	know (see 84)
klingen	klingt	klang	geklungen	sound
*kommen	kommt	kam	gekommen	come
können[7]	kann	konnte	gekonnt	can, be able to
*kriechen	kriecht	kroch	gekrochen	crawl, creep
laden	lädt[8]	lud	geladen	load; invite
lassen	läßt	ließ	gelassen	let, leave (behind)
*laufen	läuft	lief	gelaufen	run
leiden	leidet	litt	gelitten	suffer, bear
leihen	leiht	lieh	geliehen	lend
lesen	liest	las	gelesen	read
liegen	liegt	lag	gelegen	lie
lügen	lügt	log	gelogen	tell lies
messen	mißt	maß	gemessen	measure
mögen[7]	mag	mochte	gemocht	may; like
müssen[7]	muß	mußte	gemußt	must, have to
nehmen	nimmt	nahm	genommen	take

[1] See 62 (c)
[2] See 57 (a)
[3] Or hangen. Weak = hang (tr.)
[4] Weak = beat; chop
[5] See 70 (e)
[6] 70 (f)
[7] See 67
[8] Also: ladet

E

Infinitive	3rd Pers. Sing. Pres.	3rd Pers. Sing. Impf.	Past Part.	Meaning
nennen	nennt	nannte[1]	genannt	*name, call*
pfeifen	pfeift	pfiff	gepfiffen	*whistle; pipe*
preisen	preist	pries	gepriesen	*praise*
*quellen	quillt	quoll	gequollen	*spring, gush up*
raten	rät	riet	geraten	*advise; guess*
reiben	reibt	rieb	gerieben	*rub*
(*)reißen	reißt	riß	gerissen	*tear*
*reiten	reitet	ritt	geritten	*ride (on animal)*
*rennen	rennt	rannte[1]	gerannt	*run*
riechen	riecht	roch	gerochen	*smell*
ringen	ringt	rang	gerungen	*wrestle, struggle*
*rinnen	rinnt	rann	geronnen	*flow, trickle*
rufen	ruft	rief	gerufen	*call*
saufen	säuft	soff	gesoffen	*drink (of animals)*
saugen	saugt	sog	gesogen	*suck*
schaffen[2]	schafft	schuf	geschaffen	*create*
(*)scheiden	scheidet	schied	geschieden	*separate; part*
scheinen	scheint	schien	geschienen	*seem; shine*
schelten	schilt	schalt[3]	gescholten	*scold, blame*
scheren	schert	schor	geschoren	*shear, cut*
schieben	schiebt	schob	geschoben	*shove, push*
(*)schießen	schießt	schoß	geschossen	*shoot*
schinden	schindet	schund	geschunden	*flay, rub off skin*
schlafen	schläft	schlief	geschlafen	*sleep*
schlagen	schlägt	schlug	geschlagen	*beat, strike*
*schleichen	schleicht	schlich	geschlichen	*creep, slink*
schließen	schließt	schloß	geschlossen	*shut, conclude*
schlingen	schlingt	schlang	geschlungen	*coil; devour*
schmeißen	schmeißt	schmiß	geschmissen	*fling, chuck*
(*)schmelzen	schmilzt[4]	schmolz	geschmolzen	*melt*
schneiden	schneidet	schnitt	geschnitten	*cut*
schreiben	schreibt	schrieb	geschrieben	*write*
schreien	schreit	schrie	geschrie(e)n	*shout, shriek*
*schreiten	schreitet	schritt	geschritten	*stride, proceed*
schweigen	schweigt	schwieg	geschwiegen	*be(come) silent*
*schwellen[5]	schwillt	schwoll	geschwollen	*swell (intr.)*
(*)schwim-men	schwimmt	schwamm	geschwom-men[6]	*swim*
schwingen	schwingt	schwang	geschwungen	*swing*
schwören	schwört	schwur	geschworen	*swear (on oath)*
sehen	sieht	sah	gesehen	*see*

[1] See 70 (*f*).
[2] Weak = do, achieve
[3] See 70 (*e*)
[4] Also *schmelzt* when transitive
[5] Weak = swell (tr.)
[6] 57 (*c*)(*f*)

Infinitive	3rd Pers. Sing. Pres.	3rd Pers. Sing. Impf.	Past Part.	Meaning
*sein[1]	ist	war	gewesen	be
senden	sendet	sandte[2,3]	gesandt[3]	send
singen	singt	sang	gesungen	sing
*sinken	sinkt	sank	gesunken	sink (intr.)
sinnen	sinnt	sann	gesonnen	think, meditate
sitzen	sitzt	saß	gesessen	be sitting, sit
sollen[4]	soll	sollte	gesollt	be obliged to
speien	speit	spie	gespien	spit, spew out
spinnen	spinnt	spann[5]	gesponnen	spin, spin round
sprechen	spricht	sprach	gesprochen	speak
*sprießen	sprießt	sproß	gesprossen	sprout
*springen	springt	sprang	gesprungen	jump, spring
stechen	sticht	stach	gestochen	prick, sting; trump
stehen	steht	stand	gestanden	stand
stehlen	stiehlt	stahl	gestohlen	steal
*steigen	steigt	stieg	gestiegen	mount, rise
*sterben	stirbt	starb[5]	gestorben	die
*stieben	stiebt	stob	gestoben	scatter (intr.)
(*)stoßen	stößt	stieß	gestoßen	push; stumble on
(*)streichen	streicht	strich	gestrichen	stroke; wander
streiten	streitet	stritt	gestritten	argue, quarrel
tragen	trägt	trug	getragen	carry, bear; wear
treffen	trifft	traf	getroffen	meet; hit
(*)treiben	treibt	trieb	getrieben	drive, do; drift
(*)treten	tritt	trat	getreten	step, go; kick
trinken	trinkt	trank	getrunken	drink
tun	tut	tat	getan	do
(*)verderben	verdirbt	verdarb[5]	verdorben	spoil, ruin
verdrießen	verdrießt	verdroß	verdrossen	vex
vergessen	vergißt	vergaß	vergessen	forget
verlieren	verliert	verlor	verloren	lose
vermeiden	vermeidet	vermied	vermieden	avoid
*verschwin-den	verschwin-det	ver-schwand	verschwun-den	disappear
verzeihen	verzeiht	verzieh	verziehen	pardon
*wachsen	wächst	wuchs	gewachsen	grow (intr.)
waschen	wäscht	wusch	gewaschen	wash (tr.)
weben[6]	webt	wob	gewoben	weave
*weichen[7]	weicht	wich	gewichen	give way to
weisen	weist	wies	gewiesen	point, show

[1] See 57 (a)
[2] 70 (f)
[3] Also: sendete, gesendet
[4] See 67

[5] See 70 (e)
[6] Usually weak except in non-literal sense
[7] Weak = soften

Infinitive	3rd Pers. Sing. Pres.	3rd Pers. Sing. Impf.	Past Part.	Meaning
wenden	wendet	wandte[1,2]	gewandt[2]	turn (tr.)
werben	wirbt	warb[3]	geworben	woo, enlist
*werden[4]	wird	wurde	geworden	become
werfen	wirft	warf[3]	geworfen	throw
wiegen[5]	wiegt	wog	gewogen	weigh (intr.)
winden	windet	wand	gewunden	wind, twist
wissen	weiß[6]	wußte	gewußt	know (see 84)
wollen[7]	will	wollte	gewollt	want to
zeihen	zeiht	zieh	geziehen	accuse
(*)ziehen	zieht	zog	gezogen	draw, pull; grow (tr.); go, move
zwingen	zwingt	zwang	gezwungen	compel, force

[1] 70 (f)
[2] Also: wendete, gewendet
[3] See 70 (e)
[4] See 57 (a)

[5] Weak = rock
[6] See 58 (a) (vi)
[7] 67

Index

(The numbers refer to the paragraphs.)